Hindi Grammar

No more "tenses", "postpositions", "pronouns", "oblique cases", or "irregular verbs"! An innovative and long-overdue overhaul of the basic grammar of Hindi, covering rules of pronunciation, categories of word, more advanced constructions, and Hindi script, this book is ideal for beginners and especially those who have no background in languages or linguistics. It is written in a non-academic style, does not use complex terminology or irrelevant grammatical categories, and describes the grammar of a global language in a straightforward and learner-focused manner.

Learn grammar the easiest, most efficient, and least time-consuming way possible with *Hindi Grammar*.

David James Young is a lecturer in the School of Languages at Leeds Beckett University. With a deep interest in simplifying grammatical analysis, he believes strongly that language-learning materials should be accessible to *everyone*—not just those with a background in languages or linguistics.

Feedback, questions, and comments are welcome at
d.young@leedsbeckett.ac.uk.

Hindi Grammar

David James Young

Prepared and typeset by David James Young.

ISBN-13: 978-1497385252
ISBN-10: 1497385253

Also available in the same series:

Persian Grammar

Turkish Grammar

Urdu Grammar

Spanish Grammar

Latin American Spanish Grammar

European Spanish Grammar

Brazilian Portuguese Grammar

European Portuguese Grammar

for my mother

Contents

Introduction

This book is a grammar reference book. It teaches the basic, intermediate, and more advanced rules of Hindi. However, it is not just a grammar book in the traditional sense; it also covers the pronunciation of Hindi and Hindi script, and it includes a list of several hundred common words in Hindi. (Note that apart from the script, Hindi at the everyday level is mutually intelligible with Urdu; essentially, you get two languages for the price of one!)

What is grammar?

Although this book covers both the pronunciation of Hindi and Hindi script and also includes a mini-dictionary, its main focus is *grammar.* Grammar is the set of rules of any given language. Traditionally, these rules are about two things: first, the types of words that exist in a language (what are more traditionally called "nouns", "verbs", "adjectives", etc) and second, how these different types of words appear together to form meaning. There are other rules in a language; for example, there are rules for pronunciation or for how the language is written, and modern linguists also use the term "grammar" to cover these types of rules. Given this book covers the pronunciation of Hindi and Hindi script, this is a book of grammar in the modern sense; it covers the rules you will need to produce and understand Hindi.

Why is grammar important?

Grammar (in the traditional sense) is important because when learning any language, there is a clear difference between simply getting your meaning across and using the language with a degree of complexity and accuracy. If you learn the entire contents of a Hindi dictionary, you would be able to say the Hindi word for "multicultural" or "vice-president" or "hyperinflation" or any other less frequent word you can think of, but it is grammar that shows you how to put these words together into meaningful phrases. Admittedly, you could acquire a "basic knowledge" of French or Spanish for example by learning set expressions, as often occurs in modern language classes; yet, what this knowledge amounts to is often a collection of isolated phrases such as "How are you?", "I am fine, thank you", "Where is the beach?", "It is two o'clock", etc. With phrases like these, you may be able to go to France or Spain and have a limited conversation, but without some idea of grammar, you will never be able to understand why those phrases appear in the way they do or how to modify those phrases to say "Where is the supermarket?" instead of "Where is the beach?" or "No, I've had an awful day!" instead of "I am fine, thank you". At some point, all learners must learn at least some grammar.

Who is this book for?

Although this book was written for any learner of Hindi, it was designed specifically with complete beginners in mind; it assumes no prior knowledge of Hindi at all. Although learners who are already more advanced in Hindi may find they know many of the rules in this book, these learners may nevertheless find the organisation and presentation of those rules different from what they are used to; hopefully, this will be a simpler and more elegant way of organising their grammatical knowledge. This book will be particularly useful for those learners who have not learned a language before or are unsure about traditional grammatical concepts and terminology (which are simply not used). Academically, this book is suitable for the undergraduate student embarking on a South Asian Studies degree or the postgraduate student of politics or international relations learning Hindi as an elective. Students of linguistics or languages may also find the way grammar is presented in this book different from what they are used to—again, hopefully in a positive and refreshing way. Primarily though, this book was written for learners with non-academic backgrounds and motivations: learners who are studying Hindi informally in an evening class at their local college or learning independently at home in order to communicate with South Asian friends and family.

What does this book do differently?

As mentioned earlier, this book does not use traditional grammatical terminology and categories. It does not use potentially confusing (and often completely unnecessary) labels like "noun", "pronoun", "relative clause", "adverb", etc. It presents a simple grammatical system of *objects*, *helpers*, *descriptors*, and *actions*—a system which can be used to classify all words in Hindi. The rules governing each of these categories are discussed along with the rules governing how words of one category appear with words of another to impart meaning. The more complex structures of Hindi are presented as *elevations*, which is a grammatical "tool" I have developed to describe more advanced structures in a language. Finally, this book differs from other grammar books in its approach to teaching Hindi script; it presents a system wherein the number of core letters is reduced, so that what are considered letters in their own right in the traditional "scientific" description of the script are—in this book— presented simply as additional "conjunct forms". In my opinion, this is a more efficient way of actually learning the script (as opposed to just describing it).

How should this book be used?

You should work through this book slowly and methodically. Even if your knowledge of Hindi is more advanced, there may be areas of grammar that need clarification for you, and as I mentioned, this book may present grammatical categories and structures in a way you have not encountered before. Do not use the index until you have worked through the whole book. The list of words in Chapter Four and the list of elevations in Chapter Five are presented only as a "springboard" for future learning; do continue to add to these lists. The overall aim of this book is that after completing it, you will have an efficient and simple "mental framework" that you can use to organise your continued learning. What this means is that after finishing this book, you should not need to consult additional formal textbooks. What this book will not do is make you fluent in Hindi—if your definition of fluency is being able to produce and understand Hindi with very little effort. That is something that, in many ways, is entirely separate from knowing grammar; you might memorise all the rules, words, and elevations in this book (or any other book you can find on Hindi), but you would still not be able to hold a natural conversation. This is because whereas grammar is knowledge, fluency is essentially a semi-physical skill; fluency requires that you put into practice all the rules you have learned, combined with all the words and elevations you have learned, while remembering to smile and be polite—all while remembering the backstory of the

Indian soap opera you are discussing! That is something that takes practice. Finally, note that except for certain words that occur in some elevations, which you do not need to translate, all the relevant words used as examples in this book have also been included in Chapter Four.

Chapter One: Basic Rules

The rules in this chapter are the very basic rules of the language. There are five sections; the first section describes how to pronounce words in Hindi, and the remaining four sections discuss the four categories I have used to classify all words in Hindi: objects, helpers, descriptors, and actions.

Pronunciation

There are about 40 sounds in Hindi. In this book, these sounds are represented by the letters of the English alphabet. Partly because there are more sounds than there are letters to represent them, some sounds are represented by combinations of letters. The following letters represent sounds that are pronounced much the same as they are in English:

A	banana	*L*	look
Aa	father	*M*	man
Au	author	*N*	not
B	bat	*O*	hope
D	date	*Oo*	food
E	hate	*P*	pass

Ee	feet	*R*	red
Ei	head	*S*	sad
F	far	*Sh*	show
G	gate	*T*	top
H	hat	*U*	bus
I	fit	*V*	veer
J	jam	*Y*	yellow
K	calm	*Z*	zoo

Note that for convenience, before another vowel or at the end of a word, *Aa*, *Ee*, and *Oo* are written *A*, *I*, and *U* respectively. As an English speaker, you would probably pronounce *A*, *I*, and *U* like this anyway when they appear in this position:

लड़का
larka
boy ~ "*larkaa*"

आदमी
aadmi
man ~ "*aadmee*"

आलू
aalu
potato ~ "*aaloo*"

भाई
bhai
brother ~ "*bhaaee*"

One more letter can be covered very quickly: the letter *C*. This letter is pronounced as the CH of "**ch**at". The remaining sounds and the symbols used with letters are also mostly variations of the above and are discussed in Chapters Three and Six (for the time being, simply ignore any special mark, such as the dot below the *R* in "*larka*" in the above examples). In my view, the above list is probably all you need to speak Hindi for the time being—at least to a level that is intelligible.

Hindi script

Hindi is written in its own script, and this script is different from the one used in English. However, in this book, Hindi script will not be discussed until Chapter Six, after the more complex rules of Hindi have been described. In my opinion, learning the script before you learn the basic grammatical rules of Hindi ("grammatical" in the traditional sense of the word) or start to learn actual words and elevations is far more difficult than trying to learn rules, words, and elevations at the same time as you are trying to decode a completely new script. In this book, I have used a system that encodes Hindi-script spelling in the English letters used to represent Hindi sounds (though the complexities of Hindi script made it difficult to use the letters of the English alphabet in a way that I feel looked natural or was intuitively easy to use, therefore you will find some additions such as dots below letters). This means that when you do learn the script, you will know how to spell every Hindi word you have learned. Of course, if you really do want to learn Hindi script from the start, I have included a script version of all the example words and phrases given in this book. These examples will be useful to come back to and study if you learn the script at the later point I recommend:

बहिन
bahin
sister

लड़का
laṛka
boy

घर
ghar
house

किताब
kitaab
book

Objects

As mentioned earlier, every word in Hindi can be grouped into one of four categories: objects, helpers, descriptors, and actions. The system used in this book is different from traditional grammatical descriptions of languages (which use "nouns", "pronouns", "adverbs", "verbs", "adjectives", "articles", etc) because I do not want to describe an arbitrary division in any one of these categories where such a division would be (for Hindi at least) completely unnecessary. Instead of making Hindi fit traditional Latin-based framework usually used to describe it, this book concentrates on teaching the rules of Hindi in a way that is as efficient as possible. Objects are one category of word in Hindi. Objects are words that refer to things. They can be words for simple physical things like "book", "man", "cat", "city", "water", "planet", etc or more abstract things such as "anger", "intelligence", "love", "fear", etc. Words that are used to refer to other objects, such as words like "he", "she", "I", "him", "me", "us", "hers", "theirs", "ours", etc and names such as "David", "Mumbai", "England", "India", etc are also all objects. Finally, words that denote when something happened, such as "when?", "then", "never", "sometimes", words that denote where something happened, such as "where?", "there", "nowhere", "above", "out", and words that denote how something happened, such as "how?", "slowly", "definitely", "carefully", "well" are also all objects. As will be discussed later, words like "never", "there", and "slowly" are simply "shortcuts" for larger phrases built around more concrete objects: "at no *time*", "in that *place*", "in a slow *manner*", etc; therefore, there is no need to introduce another category such as "adverbs", as other grammar books might suggest.

Examples of objects

Take a look at the following examples of objects in Hindi; to keep things simple, I shall often use these basic example words when describing more complex rules:

आदमी

aadmi

man

औरत

aurat

woman

बहिन

bahin

sister

लड़का

larka

boy

घर

ghar

house

किताब

kitaab

book

लड़की

larki

girl

कमरा

kamra

room

भाई

bhai

brother

दफ़्तर

daftar

office

Helpers

Helpers are words that give meaning to other words. The only thing you need to remember about any helper is where it goes and what it means. Consider the following examples. The word "from" in English is a helper that appears before an object to denote an origin: "*from* the office", "*from* India". In Hindi, the word "*se*" is also a helper that appears with an object to denote "from"—but instead of appearing before an object, "*se*" appears after that object:

दफ़्तर से | भारत से
daftar **se** | *Bhaarat* **se**
from the office | from India

No matter what other grammar books tell you, you do not need to worry about whether this word is an "article", "determiner", "preposition", "adjective", or anything else; all you ever need to learn about the helper "*se*" is that it appears after an object and denotes "from".

Types of helper

There are many different locations helpers can appear in. A lot of helpers in Hindi appear after an object, including "*men*" – "in", "*par*" – "on", "*ke lie*" – "for", and "*ke saath*" – "with":

घर में | मेज़ पर
ghar **men** | *mez* **par**
in the house | on the table

किताब के लिए
*kitaab **ke lie***
for the book

आदमी के साथ
*aadmi **ke saath***
with the man

As you can see from these examples, an object by itself can denote "book" or "*the* book". An object by itself can also denote "*a* book", though the helper "*ek*" often appears before the object in this instance:

किताब
kitaab
book

किताब
kitaab
the book

किताब
kitaab
a book

एक किताब
***ek** kitaab*
a book

Sometimes, a helper may have a specific meaning but not a specific location. Helpers like these include "*ji haan*" – "yes", "*ji naheen*" – "no", "*dhanyavaad*" – "thank you", and "*namaste*" – "hello", and they can appear pretty much anywhere. In this case, just use them as you would in English:

जी हां
ji haan
yes

जी नहीं
ji naheen
no

धन्यवाद   नमस्ते

dhanyavaad   *namaste*

thank you   hello

The opposite may also be the case; a helper may have a specific location but not a specific meaning—at least, by itself. In Chapter Two, we shall look at ways of talking about more than one object; one way is to add the helper "...*en*" to that object. Helpers like these do not have meanings by themselves; instead, they change the meaning of the word to which they are attached:

किताब   किताबें

kitaab   *kitaaben*

book   books

Finally, note that helpers do not just appear with objects; some helpers appear with words from the other categories discussed in the following sections—or even with whole phrases. When you are learning Hindi (or any other language for that matter), you will likely read grammar books or other resources that divide helpers into a very wide variety of categories, such as "articles", "prepositions", "conjunctions", "interjections", etc. This is completely unnecessary; all you ever need to learn about any helper you encounter is where it goes and what it means.

Descriptors

Descriptors are words that describe objects. Words like "big", "small", "happy", "red", "yellow", "Indian", etc are all descriptors. Words like "eating" and "eaten", "jumping" and "jumped", "going" and "gone", etc are also descriptors, albeit slightly more complex ones. All these words are used to describe an object: "the big book", "the small dog", "the man is happy", "Indian politics", "the apple is eaten", "the man is not going", etc.

Two types of phrase

Descriptors can appear in two types of phrase. The first type of phrase is "the big book", "the happy man", "red apples", "British people", etc, where the descriptor—in English at least—appears before an object. To form phrases like these in Hindi, the descriptor also appears before an object, just as in English:

अच्छा

accha

good

अच्छा आदमी

accha aadmi

the good man

जवान

javaan

young

जवान लड़का

javaan laṛka

the young boy

The second type of phrase is "the book is big", "the man is happy", "apples are red", "the people are British", etc. To form phrases like these, descriptors appear with a word like "is", "was", or "will be". We shall look at how to say "is", "was", and "will be" in Chapter Two; for now, just remember that the word "*hei*" in the following examples means "is" and appears right at the end of the phrase:

आदमी अच्छा है   लड़का जवान है

aadmi accha hei   *laṛka javaan hei*

the man is good   the boy is young

Finally, note the difference between words like "careful" and "carefully" or "quiet" and "quietly". The former are descriptors, but the latter—because they describe how something was done—are objects. As I mentioned before, words like "carefully" or "quietly" are really just "shortcuts"; instead of saying a full phrase like "he went into the kitchen in a quiet manner", we just say "he went into the kitchen *quietly*". The phrase "in a quiet manner" means exactly the same thing as "quietly", and at its heart is an object: "manner" (linguists call this a "noun phrase"). From this, it is a simple enough step to then call the word "quietly" an object, given that it means the exact same thing. Likewise, the word "when?" can also be described as object because it is really just a shortcut for "at what point in *time*?", "never" is an object because it is a shortcut for "at no point in *time*", "where?" is an object because it is a shortcut for "at what *place*?", and "why?" is an object because it is a shortcut for "for what *reason*?" etc.

Actions

Actions are words that refer, evidently, to actions. These actions can be simple physical actions like "run", "jump", "see", "think", etc or more abstract actions like "be", "become", "have", "seem", etc. Actions in Hindi are very regular; apart from some very limited exceptions, after learning each action, you will be able to form all the different expressions associated with that action, such as "will see", "saw", "used to see", etc. This is not the case in some other languages—such as English and French—in which you need to learn more than one form for each action (compare "do", "did", and "done" or "see", "saw", and "seen" etc in English). Note also that no matter what other grammar books might suggest, there is no need to learn something called the "infinitive" form: *"dekhna"* – "to see", *"jaana"* – "to go", *"khaana"* – "to eat", etc. The "infinitive" form is often not best described as an action at all—but as an object, and standard translations of the "infinitive" can often be problematic.

Helpers that appear with actions

A small set of helpers appear with actions to denote when an action happens; these helpers all appear after the action. These helpers are *"hei"*, *"ho"*, *"ga"*, *"tha"*, *"...ta"*, *"...a"*, and *"...e"*. More than one of these helpers can appear; for example, to denote that the action happens regularly, the combination *"...ta hei"* is added:

बोल

bol

speak

आदमी बोलता है

*aadmi bol**ta hei***

the man speaks

The following helpers—or combinations of helpers—are used to denote other times. Other combinations are used in very specific phrases, but these will be discussed in Chapter Five; the following helpers are all you need for the moment:

आदमी बोला
aadmi bola
the man spoke

आदमी बोले गा
aadmi bole ga
the man will speak

आदमी बोला है
aadmi bola hei
the man has spoken

आदमी बोला था
aadmi bola tha
the man had spoken

आदमी बोलता था
aadmi bolta tha
the man used to speak

Note that this description of actions is not the approach you will find in other grammar resources; this book does not use labels such as the "present tense", "past tense", "subjunctive", etc. In my view, just like dividing objects and helpers into unnecessary categories, referring to "tenses" is needlessly confusing. Simply associating every "tense" you learn in Hindi with an equivalent English phrase is a much easier approach than learning complex labels like "present perfect continuous passive"—and then going on to translate anyway! You can be confident that if you only learn the few examples given above (which takes all of ten minutes), you will know the "present simple", "past simple", "future simple", "present perfect", "past perfect", and "past habitual" in Hindi!

Once you have learned this core set of helpers, it is simple enough to substitute other actions for "*bol*":

देख

dekh

see

आदमी देखता है

*aadmi **dekh**ta hei*

the man sees

लिख

likh

write

लड़का लिखता है

*laṛka **likh**ta hei*

the boy writes

When you do substitute other actions, note that if two vowels come together, a *Y* is inserted between them:

सो

so

sleep

लड़का सोया

laṛka soya

the boy slept

Finally, note that as you may have noticed from the examples above, the object denoting who performs an action appears before that action (as in English). However, in Hindi, anything else appears between the two. In Hindi, you say something like "the man *from the office* comes" for "the man comes from the office":

आदमी दफ्तर से आता है

*aadmi **daftar se** aata hei*

the man comes from the office

Chapter Two: Elementary Rules

The rules in this chapter expand upon the more basic rules discussed in the previous chapter. There are four sections; each section discusses additional rules about one category of word (objects, helpers, descriptors, and actions respectively).

Objects: Talking about more than one thing

There are specific rules you should use if you are talking about more than one thing (i.e. if you want to say "books" instead of "book", "men" instead of "man", etc). The basic rule about talking about more than one thing is simply to use the same form as when talking about one thing, as follows:

आदमी
aadmi
man

आदमी
aadmi
men

सेब
seb
apple

सेब
seb
apples

However, this is not always the case; if an object ends in *A*, this changes to *E*:

लड़का

larka

boy

लड़के

larke

boys

केला

kela

banana

केले

kele

bananas

कमरा

kamra

room

कमरे

kamre

rooms

To an extent (and as often happens in languages), this change is "reflected" in other types of words; if an accompanying descriptor ends in the letter *A*, this also becomes *E*:

अच्छा आदमी

accha aadmi

the good man

अच्छे आदमी

acche aadmi

the good men

लड़का अच्छा है

larka accha hei

the boy is good

लड़के अच्छे हैं

larke acche hein

the boys are good

A similar change takes place when more than one thing performs an action; in this instance, change any letter *A* in the helpers that occur after that action to *E*. To any other vowel, add *N*:

आदमी बोलता है
aadmi bolta hei
the man speaks

आदमी बोलते हैं
aadmi bolte hein
the men speak

आदमी बोले गा
aadmi bole ga
the man will speak

आदमी बोलें गे
aadmi bolen ge
the men will speak

Note that before certain helpers like *"men"* – "in", *"par"* – "on", *"se"* – "from", *"ke lie"* – "for", an object acts as though it denoted more than one thing. Other grammar books may describe these objects with complex labels like "declensions" or "oblique cases" (they may even describe *any* object with a helper in these terms)—this is absolutely unnecessary.   Just remember that objects act as if they denoted more than one thing before certain helpers. You can find a list of these helpers in Chapter Four—they always appear after an object, and in the lists in Chapter Four, they are listed under the heading "Helpers that appear after objects":

लड़के
larke
boys

लड़के के लिए
larke ke lie
for the **boy**

कमरे

kamre

rooms

अच्छे कमरे में

acche kamre men

in the good **room**

बच्चे

bacce

children

अच्छे बच्चे के लिए

acche bacce ke lie

for the good **child**

If an object in such a position actually does denote more than one thing, either add "*...on*" or change any final *E* to "*...on*":

घर

ghar

houses

घरों के लिए

*ghar**on** ke lie*

for the houses

कमरे

kamre

rooms

अच्छे कमरों में

*acche kamr**on** men*

in the good rooms

बच्चे

bacce

children

अच्छे बच्चों के लिए

*acche bacc**on** ke lie*

for the good children

Talking about women

There are also specific rules you should use if you are talking about women. If an object denotes a woman, add "...*en*" to denote more than one woman:

औरत

aurat

woman

औरतें

*aurat**en***

women

बहिन

bahin

sister

बहिनें

*bahin**en***

sisters

However, if an object that denotes a woman ends in the letter *I*, replace this with "...*iyaan*":

लड़की

laṛki

girl

लड़कियां

*laṛk**iyaan***

girls

पत्नी

patni

wife

पत्नियां

*patn**iyaan***

wives

Like the changes described in the previous section, this change is also "reflected" in other types of words, as detailed below.

If an accompanying descriptor ends in the letter *A*, this becomes *I*:

अच्छा आदमी
accha aadmi
the good man

अच्छी औरत
acchi aurat
the good woman

आदमी अच्छा है
aadmi accha hei
the man is good

औरत अच्छी है
aurat acchi hei
the woman is good

Similarly, when a woman performs an action, change any letter *A* in the helpers that occur after that action to *I*:

आदमी बोलता है
aadmi bolta hei
the man speaks

औरत बोलती है
aurat bolti hei
the woman speaks

आदमी बोले गा
aadmi bole ga
the man will speak

औरत बोले गी
aurat bole gi
the woman will speak

Both changes still apply if more than one woman is denoted:

अच्छे आदमी बोलते हैं
acche aadmi bolte hein
the good men speak

अच्छी औरतें बोलती हैं
acchi auraten bolti hein
the good women speak

अच्छे आदमी बोलें गे
acche aadmi bolen ge
the good men will speak

अच्छी औरतें बोलें गी
acchi auraten bolen gi
the good women will speak

However, the helpers "*tha*" and "*...a*" also add *N* when more than one woman is denoted:

आदमी बोले
aadmi bole
the men spoke

औरतें बोलीं
auraten boleen
the women spoke

आदमी बोलते थे
aadmi bolte the
the men used to speak

औरतें बोलती थीं
auraten bolti theen
the women used to speak

It is important to get these particular changes right because—as will be described in the next chapter—Hindi has objects like "*vo*", which can mean "he", "she", "it", or "they"! With objects like these, the main way of showing that you mean "he" instead of "she" or "they" instead of "he" etc is by these changes:

वह जाता है
vo jaata hei
he goes

वह जाती है
vo jaati hei
she goes

वे जाते हैं
vo jaate hein
they go

वे जाती हैं
vo jaati hein
they go ~denoting women

Finally, note that objects denoting women never act as if they denoted more than one thing before helpers like "*men*" – "in", "*par*" – "on", "*se*" – "from", "*ke lie*" – "for", etc:

लड़के के लिए
larke ke lie
for the boy

लड़की के लिए
larki ke lie
for the girl

अच्छे लड़के से
acche larke se
from the good boy

अच्छी लड़की से
acchi larki se
from the good girl

However, the helpers "*…en*" and "*…iyaan*" change to "*…on*" and "*…iyon*" respectively, which reflects a similar change to other objects:

घरों के लिए
gharon ke lie
for the houses

लड़कों से
larkon se
from the boys

औरतें
auraten
women

औरतों के लिए
auraton ke lie
for the women

लड़कियां
larkiyaan
girls

लड़कियों से
larkiyon se
from the girls

Helpers: "is", "was", "will be"

Contrary to what you might expect, to say "is", "was", "will be", etc, you do not actually use an action at all; instead, you use some of the helpers that come after actions—but without any accompanying action. Specifically, you use: *"hei"*, *"tha"*, and the combination *"ho ga"*, as follows:

आदमी अच्छा है
*aadmi accha **hei***
the man is good

आदमी अच्छा था
*aadmi accha **tha***
the man was good

आदमी अच्छा हो गा
*aadmi accha **ho ga***
the man will be good

लड़का एक आदमी हो गा
*larka ek aadmi **ho ga***
the boy will be a man

All the changes described in the previous two sections still apply, just as if there actually was an action present:

आदमी अच्छे हैं
*aadmi acche **hein***
the men are good

औरतें अच्छी थीं
*auraten acchi **theen***
the women were good

लड़के अच्छे हों गे
*larke acche **hon ge***
the boys will be good

लड़कियां औरतें हों गी
*larkiyaan auraten **hon gi***
the girls will be women

Descriptors: Numbers

In Hindi, numbers are best described as descriptors; they can appear by themselves (when counting for example) or before an object—just like other descriptors:

एक, दो, तीन, चार
ek, do, teen, caar
one, two, three, four

दो किताबें
do *kitaaben*
two books

However, compared to numbers in other languages, numbers in Hindi are admittedly a little difficult. This is not because there are lots of rules about them; rather, it is because numbers in Hindi are not *constructed*. In English, most numbers from 20 up are constructed: you say "twenty one", "twenty two", "fifty six", "seventy seven", etc. Constructed numbers are formed by combinations of *unique* numbers such as "one", "seven", "seventy", "hundred", etc, and once you have learned the limited set of *unique* numbers, you can form any other constructed number. In English, there are about 28 unique numbers—in Hindi, however, all numbers from one to 100 are unique! What this means it that essentially, you just have to learn these numbers individually (there is a list in Chapter Four):

दो
do
two

सात
saat
seven

सोलह
solah
sixteen

चौंतीस
cauntees
thirty four

अड़तालीस

aṛtaalees

forty eight

सत्तानवे

sattaanve

ninety seven

सौ

sau

hundred

हज़ार

hazaar

thousand

All other numbers are constructed through combinations of the above words, as follows:

दो सौ अड़तालीस

do sau aṛtaalees

two hundred and forty eight

सात सौ सोलह

saat sau solah

seven hundred and sixteen

सात हज़ार दो सौ सत्तानवे

saat hazaar do sau sattaanve

seven thousand two hundred and ninety seven

अड़तालीस हज़ार सात सौ दो

aṛtaalees hazaar saat sau do

forty-eight thousand seven hundred and two

Actions: Actions with *"mein"* and *"tum"*

The objects *"mein"* – "I" and *"tum"* – "you" have an effect on helpers that appear after actions; with *"mein"*, start with the default forms, and any vowel other than *A* becomes *OoN*:

आदमी बोलता है
aadmi bolta hei
the man speaks

मैं बोलता हूं
mein bolta hoon
I speak

आदमी बोले गा
aadmi bole ga
the man will speak

मैं बोलूं गा
mein boloon ga
I will speak

आदमी यहां है
aadmi yahaan hei
the man is here

मैं यहां हूं
mein yahaan hoon
I am here

आदमी अच्छा था
aadmi accha tha
the man was good

मैं अच्छा था
mein accha tha
I was good

Likewise, with *"tum"*, start with the default forms, and any vowel other than *A* becomes *O* (note that *"tum"* most often denotes more than one person, as will be clarified in the next chapter):

आदमी बोलता है
aadmi bolta hei
the man speaks

तुम बोलते हो
tum bolte ho
you speak

आदमी बोले गा
aadmi bole ga
the man will speak

तुम बोलो गे
tum bolo ge
you will speak

आदमी यहां है
aadmi yahaan hei
the man is here

तुम यहां हो
tum yahaan ho
you are here

आदमी अच्छा था
aadmi accha tha
the man was good

तुम अच्छे थे
tum acche the
you were good

Other grammar books will use the terms "first person", "second person", and "third person". These are terms for describing respectively the person speaking, the person spoken to, and the person spoken about. A lot is made of these differences in many language books, but in my view, the changes that occur to actions depending on "person" can be simply described as exceptions that occur with certain objects—the fact that in any given language, these objects are often some of the most frequently used does not necessitate three structural categories (in Arabic at least, although this three-way system is still a part of traditional grammatical description, the "third person" is considered the "default" form). There is literally an infinite number of objects that do *not* cause "first person" or "second person" forms to be created, compared with the two or three objects that do! In my view, a more efficient way of describing these forms is simply to say that when a specific, limited number of objects are used with actions, the action changes in some way from the default (i.e. "third person") form. In Hindi, the objects "*mein*" and "*tum*" cause these special changes, and that's all you need to remember.

Chapter Three: Intermediate Rules

Now that we have discussed the basic and elementary rules of Hindi, we are ready to look at the more intermediate rules of Hindi. There are five sections in this chapter; the first four sections each discuss additional rules about one category of word (objects, helpers, descriptors, and actions respectively), while the last section discusses additional rules about pronunciation.

Objects: Troublemakers

As in many languages, we can think of certain objects in Hindi as *troublemakers*; what I mean is that whenever there is a special rule or exception, it often involves one of these objects! The good news is that there aren't that many of these objects in Hindi; the bad news of course is that these are the objects you will use very frequently in almost every conversation you have. (Often, high-frequency words in languages have special rules associated with them; being used all the time, they are more apt to "mutate".) We encountered two troublemakers in the previous chapter: *"mein"* and *"tum"*—but there is also *"ham"*, *"ye"*, *"vo"*, *"tu"*, *"kaun?"*, *"kya?"*, *"jo"*, and *"koi"*. First, let's look at the meaning of each of these objects.

The objects *"mein"* and *"ham"* are straightforward: *"mein"* means "I" (as mentioned previously), and *"ham"* means "we":

मैं बोलता हूं
mein bolta hoon
I speak

हम बोलते हैं
ham bolte hein
we speak

Note that in spoken Hindi, you will often hear speakers use "ham" for "mein"—in this instance, the action still acts as though it denotes more than one thing (i.e. you still say "we"):

मैं बोलता हूं
mein bolta hoon
I speak

हम बोलते हैं
ham bolte hein
I speak ~in spoken Hindi

The objects *"vo"* and *"ye"* are a little more complex; as was also mentioned previously, *"vo"* can denote "he", "she", "it" or "they"—but only when what you are talking about is *distant*:

वह बोलती है
vo bolti hei
she speaks ~the woman who is distant

वे बोलते हैं
vo bolte hein
they speak ~the men who are distant

We have a similar situation in English with "this" and "that"; "this" is usually used when something is near to you, and "that" is usually used when something is further away. Of course, there is no specific measurement—the distance of the object is relative. In fact, the word "*vo*" in Hindi can also mean "that" or "those":

वह अच्छा लगता है
vo *accha lagta hei*
that seems good

वे अच्छे लगते हैं
vo *acche lagte hein*
those seem good

The object "*ye*" is very similar to "*vo*"; it also denotes "he", "she", "it", and "they"—but only when these objects are *near* (again, relatively speaking); likewise, it can also denote "this" or "these":

यह बोलता है
ye *bolta hei*
he speaks ~the man who is near

ये बोलती हैं
ye *bolti hein*
they speak ~the women who are near

यह अच्छा लगता है
ye *accha lagta hei*
this seems good

ये अच्छे लगते हैं
ye *acche lagte hein*
these seem good

In practice, you can often just use "*vo*" to denote "he" or "she", since you would usually use names to refer to anyone near you.

The objects *"tu"*, *"tum"*, and *"aap"* all denote "you". Here is a clear indication that Hindi belongs to the same "family" as many European languages—compare the *"tu"* of Hindi with the *"tu"* of the Romance languages, the *"du"* of German and the Scandinavian languages, the "thou" of English, and the "تو" of Persian; there are also equivalents in the Slavic and Gaelic languages. Very simply, the object *"tu"* denotes one person, while the object *"tum"* (often occurring with *"log"* in this instance) denotes more than one person:

तू बोलता है
tu bolta hei
you speak ~talking to one person

तुम लोग बोलते हो
tum log bolte ho
you speak ~talking to more than one person

As in many of the languages just mentioned, the situation in Hindi has been complicated by the desire to be polite; the version of "you" that originally denoted more than one person is eventually used to denote respect to a single person (perhaps by implying that the person you are talking to is important: "you *and your retinue*", in a similar manner to kings and queens saying "we" instead of "I"). This eventually becomes the more standard form (because everyone wants to be polite)—until the original "you" that denoted one person is only used in a limited set of circumstances (think of when you would ever use "thou" in English). In Hindi, the object *"tu"* is still used to address one person, but it is usually only used with your own child, close friend, loved one, or pet (God is also addressed with *"tu"*)—or to imply that the person you are addressing has a lower status, such as a servant or a person you want to insult. For this reason, it is probably best to avoid *"tu"* in all instances until you are more confident in Hindi. Given that *"tu"* is only used to address a limited number of people, the object *"tum"* has taken its place and has come to be used to address one person (in exactly the same way that "you" is now used in English instead of "thou"; it's just the process in Hindi is not yet "complete"). In this instance, it is used neutrally; *"tum"* is not especially polite, but neither is it especially familiar or rude. However, it is important to remember that however you use it, *"tum"* must still act grammatically as though it still denoted more than one person:

तुम बोलते हो
tum bolte ho
you speak ~talking to one person

The situation with *"tu"* and *"tum"* has become even more complex in Hindi because there is in fact a third way of saying "you"—the object *"aap"*. This object may be used when you are talking either to one person or more than one person, and using it means you are showing respect to the person or people addressed. As such, until you are more confident in Hindi, it is probably simpler just to use *"aap"* in most situations (at the very worst, you may sound a little formal). As with *"tum"*, *"aap"* always acts grammatically as though it denoted more than one person:

आप बोलते हैं
aap bolte hein
you speak ~talking to one person

Our remaining troublemakers are fairly straightforward; *"kaun?"* denotes "who?", and *"kya?"* denotes "what?"—note also the position of question words like these near the action:

घर में कौन है?
*Ghar men **kaun** hei?*
Who is in the house?

घर में क्या है?
*Ghar men **kya** hei?*
What is in the house?

The object *"koi"* denotes "someone":

कोई घर में है
***koi** ghar men hei*
someone is in the house

The object *"jo"* denotes "who"—but not the version of "who" that is used in questions; it can also denote "that" or "which":

वह आदमी जो घर में है
*vo aadmi **jo** ghar men hei*
the man who is in the house

वह किताब जो घर में है
vo kitaab jo ghar men hei
the book **that** is in the house

वह किताब जो घर में है
vo kitaab jo ghar men hei
the book, **which** is in the house

So, why are these objects troublemakers? In the previous chapter, I described how certain helpers made the objects they come after act as though they denoted more than one thing:

लड़के

larke

boys

लड़के से

larke se

from the **boy**

कमरे

kamre

rooms

कमरे में

kamre men

in the **room**

When troublemakers appear before helpers like these, they change forms; for example, the object "*mein*" changes to "*mujh*":

मुझ से

mujh *se*

from me

मुझ पर

mujh *par*

on me

Note that here, "*mein*" has been translated as "me". This is in fact a consequence of a similar rule in English; in English, the object "I" changes after a helper—we say "from *me*" and "on *me*" and not the jarring-sounding "from I" or "on I". Similarly, "he" changes to "him", "they" changes to "them", "we" changes to "us", etc. This is exactly what is happening in Hindi when "*mein*" changes to "*mujh*", and any instance of "*mein se*" or "*mein par*" etc would sound equally jarring.

In a similar manner to *"mein"*, the object *"tu"* changes to *"tujh"*:

तुझ से
***tujh** se*
from you

तुझ पर
***tujh** par*
on you

The object *"ye"* changes to *"is"* if it denotes one thing and *"in"* if it denotes more than one thing; likewise, *"vo"* changes to *"us"* if it denotes one thing and *"un"* if it denotes more than one thing:

इस से
***is** se*
from him

इन पर
***in** par*
on these

उस से
***us** se*
from that

उन पर
***un** par*
on them

Similarly, the object *"kaun?"* and *"kya?"* both change to *"kis?"* if they denote one thing and *"kin?"* if they denote more than one thing; *"jo"* changes to *"jis"* and *"jin"*:

किस से
***kis** se?*
from whom?

किन पर
***kin** par?*
on whom?

जिस से
***jis** se*
from which

जिन पर
***jin** par*
on whom

Finally, "*koi*" changes to "*kisi*":

किसी से   किसी पर

kisi se   *kisi* par

from someone   on someone

These special forms may seem a lot to learn, but it is actually fairly easy to do so because you will encounter them all the time—you will never hear a native speaker not use them.

Helpers: Combinations with "*ko*"

The helper "*ko*" denotes "to" and appears after any object:

वह आदमी को किताब देता है

*vo aadmi **ko** kitaab deta hei*

he gives the book to the man

However, when the helper "*ko*" appears with some of the troublemakers described in the previous section, both helper and object combine into a new form; for example, the object "*mein*" and the helper "*ko*" combine into "*mujhe*":

वह मुझे किताब देता है

*vo **mujhe** kitaab deta hei*

he gives the book to me

The object *"ham"* and the helper *"ko"* combine into *"hamen"*:

वह हमें किताब देता है
vo **hamen** kitaab deta hei
he gives the book to us

The object *"tu"* and the helper *"ko"* combine into *"tujhe"*, while *"tum"* and *"ko"* combine into *"tumhen"*:

वह तुझे किताब देता है
vo **tujhe** kitaab deta hei
he gives the book to you

वह तुम्हें किताब देता है
vo **tumhen** kitaab deta hei
he gives the book to you

The object *"vo"* and the helper *"ko"* combine into *"use"* if they denote one thing and *"unhen"* if more than one thing:

आप उसे किताब देते हैं
aap **use** kitaab dete hein
you give the book to him

आप उन्हें किताब देते हैं
aap **unhen** kitaab dete hein
you give the book to them

Similar changes occur with *"ye"*, *"jo"*, and *"kaun?"*:

आप इसे किताब देते हैं
aap **ise** kitaab dete hein
you give the book to him

आप इन्हें किताब देते हैं
aap **inhen** kitaab dete hein
you give the book to them

वह आदमी जिसे आप किताब देते हैं
*vo aadmi **jise** aap kitaab dete hein*
the man to whom you give the book

वे आदमी जिन्हें आप किताब देते हैं
*vo aadmi **jinhen** aap kitaab dete hein*
the men to whom you give the book

आप किताब किसे देते हैं
*Aap kitaab **kise** dete hein?*
To whom do you give the book? ~which person?

आप किताब किन्हें देते हैं
*Aap kitaab **kinhen** dete hein?*
To whom do you give the book? ~which people?

These combined forms with *"ko"* (unlike the combinations with *"ka"* described in the next section) are essentially optional—it is also possible to use the uncombined forms, though this is much less common:

वह मुझे किताब देता है   वह मुझ को किताब देता है
vo mujhe kitaab deta hei   *vo **mujh ko** kitaab deta hei*
he gives the book to me   he gives the book to me

Finally, note that the special forms in this section—*"inhen"*, *"unhen"*, *"jinhen"*, and *"kinhen"*—all end in nasal *N*s.

Combinations with "*ka*"

When studying another language, there are often words that are difficult or impossible to translate; in my view, it is often misleading even to try to translate these words. The helper "*ka*" is such a word. It is possible to translate this helper as "of", as in phrases such as "the book *of* the man" etc; however, this is problematic because the order in which the two associated objects occur is different in Hindi. A more apt translation might be the "apostrophe S" of English phrases like "the man*'s* book" (though this is also problematic as in certain phrases, there is sometimes no following object). In my view, it is simpler to consider the helper "*ka*" as untranslatable; what this means is you simply learn how to use the word without worrying about a direct translation. Essentially, when the helper "*ka*" appears between two objects, it denotes that the second object belongs to the first:

आदमी का सेब
*aadmi **ka** seb*
the man's apple / the apple of the man

लड़की का घर
*laṛki **ka** ghar*
the girl's house / the house of the girl

Note that the helper "*ka*" is one of those helpers that makes the previous object act as though it denoted more than one thing:

लड़के का सेब	लड़कों का घर
laṛke ka seb	*laṛkon ka ghar*
the **boy's** apple	the **boys'** house

As with *"ko"*, when the helper *"ka"* appears with some of the troublemakers described in the previous section, both helper and object combine into a new form; for example, the object *"mein"* and the helper *"ka"* combine into *"mera"*. Given that *"mein"* means *"I"*, the new form *"mera"* can be translated as "my":

मेरा सेब
mera seb
my apple

The object *"ham"* and the helper *"ka"* combine into *"hamaara"*:

हमारा सेब
hamaara seb
our apple

The object *"tu"* and the helper *"ka"* combine into *"tera"*, while *"tum"* and *"ka"* combine into *"tumhaara"*:

तेरा सेब
tera seb
your apple

तुम्हारा सेब
tumhaara seb
your apple

Other troublemakers do not combine with *"ka"*:

इसका सेब
is ka seb
his apple

आपका सेब
aap ka seb
your apple

The changes that occur when talking about more than one thing or when talking about women are also reflected in the helper "*ka*". If the object that follows "*ka*" denotes more than one thing, the *A* of "*ka*" becomes *E*; similarly, if the object that follows denotes a woman—or women—the *A* becomes *I*, as follows:

आदमी का कमरा

aadmi ka kamra

the man's room

आदमी के कमरे

aadmi ke kamre

the man's rooms

आदमी की बहिन

aadmi ki bahin

the man's sister

आदमी की बहिनें

aadmi ki bahinen

the man's sisters

These changes have a subsequent effect on the special combined forms, as follows:

मेरे भाई

mere bhai

my brothers

हमारे भाई

hamaare bhai

our brothers

तेरी बहिन

teri bahin

your sister

तुम्हारी बहिनें

tumhaari bahinen

your sisters

These special combined forms with "*ka*" also occur whenever "*ka*" appears as an independent part of another helper. The helper "*ke lie*", for example, is really made up of the helper "*ka*" (appearing here as "*ke*") followed by the word "*lie*". It is not necessary to know what the word "*lie*" means—just remember that this helper means "for" and appears after an object:

आदमी के लिए
*aadmi **ke lie***
for the man

औरत के लिए
*aurat **ke lie***
for the woman

With helpers like these, combined forms are still produced:

आदमी के लिए
aadmi ke lie
for the man

मेरे लिए
***mere** lie*
for me

आदमी की तरफ़
aadmi ki taraf
toward the man

हमारी तरफ़
***hamaari** taraf*
toward us

आदमी के ऊपर
aadmi ke oopar
above the man

तेरे ऊपर
***tere** oopar*
above you

आदमी के साथ
aadmi ke saath
with the man

तुम्हारे साथ
***tumhaare** saath*
with you

Descriptors: "seventh", "eighth", "ninth"

To say "seventh" instead of "seven" or "fourteenth" instead of "fourteen" etc, simply add the helper "...*vaan*" to any number:

सात

saat
seven

सातवां

*saat**vaan***
seventh

सतासी

sataasi
eighty seven

सतासीवां

*sataasee**vaan***
eighty seventh

If the following object is a woman, "...*vaan*" changes to "...*veen*":

सातवां आदमी

saatvaan aadmi
the seventh man

सातवीं औरत

*saat**veen** aurat*
the seventh woman

When describing an object that is acting as though it denoted more than one thing, "...*vaan*" changes to "...*ven*":

सातवें आदमी के लिए

*saat**ven** aadmi ke lie*
for the seventh man

सातवें कमरे में

*saat**ven** kamre men*
in the seventh room

In English, we don't always say "X^(th)", as in "7^(th)" or "56^(th)" etc; with some numbers, we have to say "X^(rd)", as in "3^(rd)" or "83^(rd)", or "X^(nd)", as in "2^(nd)" or "92^(nd)" etc. The same situation exists in Hindi—albeit to a more limited extent.   To say "first", "second", "third", "fourth", "sixth", or "ninth", use the following special forms:

पहला आदमी
pahla aadmi
the first man

दूसरा आदमी
doosra aadmi
the second man

तीसरा आदमी
teesra aadmi
the third man

चौथा आदमी
cautha aadmi
the fourth man

छठा आदमी
chaṭha aadmi
the sixth man

नवां आदमी
navaan aadmi
the ninth man

Being descriptors that end in *A*, these numbers change as normal; "*navaan*" also changes like "*...vaan*":

तीसरे आदमी से
teesre aadmi se
from the third man

दूसरी लड़की
doosri laṛki
the second girl

नवीं औरत
naveen aurat
the ninth woman

नवें लड़के से
naven laṛke se
from the ninth boy

Actions: Special actions

As mentioned earlier, actions in Hindi are quite regular. Compared to many other languages (especially the languages some readers might be more familiar with, like French, Spanish, and German), there are very few "special" actions in Hindi—by which I mean actions that have exceptional rules associated with them. I do not want to use the term "irregular", which is used in many other grammar books; in my view, there are no truly irregular actions in Hindi, just as there are no (or very few) irregular actions in many of the other languages in which this label is applied. In fact, there are only six special actions in Hindi: *"de"* – "give", *"ho"* – "become", *"ja"* – "go", *"kar"* – "do", *"le"* – "take", and *"pi"* – "drink". Like the troublemakers described earlier (and for the same reason), these are some of the most frequently used actions in the language. Many of the special rules associated with these actions involve the helper *"...a"*; for example, when appearing with this helper, the action *"ja"* becomes *"gay"*:

आदमी जाता है
aadmi jaata hei
the man goes

आदमी गया
*aadmi **gaya***
the man went

The actions *"de"*, *"kar"*, *"le"*, and *"pi"* become *"diy"*, *"kiy"*, *"liy"*, and *"piy"* respectively (note that the following examples contain the helper *"ne"*—this word is explained in Chapter Five):

आदमी देता है
aadmi deta hei
the man gives

आदमी ने दिया
*aadmi ne **diya***
the man gave

आदमी करता है
aadmi karta hei
the man does

आदमी ने किया
*aadmi ne **kiya***
the man did

आदमी लेता है
aadmi leta hei
the man takes

आदमी ने लिया
*aadmi ne **liya***
the man took

आदमी पीता है
aadmi peeta hei
the man drinks

आदमी ने पिया
*aadmi ne **piya***
the man drank

The action "*ho*" becomes "*hu*":

आदमी होता है
aadmi hota hei
the man becomes

आदमी हुआ
*aadmi **hu**a*
the man became

Any changes that occur if you are talking about women or more than one thing are also reflected in the new forms:

आदमी हुआ
aadmi hua
the man became

आदमी हुए
aadmi hue
the men became

औरत गई
*aurat gay**i***
the woman went

औरतें गईं
*auraten gay**een***
the women went

As is the case with *"ka"* and *"ke lie"*, if the helper *"...a"* appears in combination with another helper, the same changes still occur:

आदमी बोला है
aadmi bola hei
the man has spoken

आदमी गया है
*aadmi **gaya** hei*
the man has gone

आदमी बोला था
aadmi bola tha
the man had spoken

आदमी ने किया था
*aadmi ne **kiya** tha*
the man had done

There is one final change that occurs with the actions *"de"* and *"le"*; when the helper *"...e"* is added to one of these actions, the final *E* of *"de"* and *"le"* is dropped:

आदमी दे गा
aadmi de ga
the man will give

आदमी दें गे
aadmi den ge
the men will give

आदमी ले गा
aadmi le ga
the man will take

आदमी लें गे
aadmi len ge
the men will take

मैं दूं गा
mein doon ga
I will give

तुम लो गे
tum lo ge
you will take

Pronunciation: Sounds pronounced in two different ways

A peculiar feature of Hindi (at least, for most English speakers) is the fact that there are several sounds that are pronounced in two different ways. For example, the letter T is pronounced in English with the tongue somewhere just above the top teeth; however, in Hindi, there are two versions of T, depending on where the tongue is positioned relative to English. In one version, the tongue is further toward the teeth than in English, and in the other version, the tongue is further away from the teeth than in English; the latter is always the less frequent version of these sounds, and linguists have predicted that these versions were adopted into Hindi from surrounding languages; many of the English words that are used in Hindi are also pronounced this way.

Let's start with the letter *T*. In Chapter One, I said that the letter *T* was pronounced as in English. For basic communication, you can do this; however, as I mentioned, this letter is in fact pronounced in one of two ways. The first pronunciation involves the tongue definitely touching the teeth. Say the T of an English word like "team" and notice that your tongue is touching the ridge just behind your teeth. Instead of placing it here, put your tongue directly between your teeth—just as if you are saying the TH of words like "think", but don't let the air through in a hiss as you would do with TH. In Hindi, by default, pronounce any *T* you encounter between the teeth like this:

तेरी बहिन
teri bahin
your sister

वह तैरता है
vo teirta hei
he swims

The second way of pronouncing T may actually be easier, although it will perhaps sound stranger to English ears. For the second version, instead of placing your tongue on your teeth or on the ridge just behind your teeth as in English, avoid your teeth altogether and put your tongue on the roof of your mouth. Again, say the word "team" as normal, but make sure the tip of your tongue is touching the roof of your mouth. As I mentioned, this is the less frequent pronunciation of *T* in Hindi, so in this book, it appears as the letter *T* with a dot beneath it, as follows:

होटल

hoṭal

hotel

ऊंट

oonṭ

camel

The same variation applies to the letter D. In the first version of *D*, the tongue touches the teeth, and in the second, the tongue touches the roof of the mouth. When the tongue touches the teeth, this should almost sound like the TH of "though". Again, by default, pronounce any *D* you encounter in this way. Likewise, for the second version of *D*, put your tongue on the roof of your mouth, behind the ridge that is just above your teeth; as with *T*, this may sound stranger than the first version of this letter. The first version of *D* is also more frequent and is denoted by a letter *D* as normal; the second version is denoted by *D* with a dot beneath it, as follows:

दोस्त

dost

friend

दिन

din

day

The first version of *D* is also more frequent and is denoted by a letter *D* as normal; the second version is denoted by *D* with a dot beneath it, as follows:

अंडा

anḍa

egg

पोलैंड

Poleinḍ

Poland

The situation with *T* and *D* is mirrored exactly with the letter *R*; in one version, the tongue touches the teeth, and in the second version, the tongue touches the roof of the mouth. The first version of *R* is "rolled" or "trilled", much as it is in Italian and Spanish. If you have a problem rolling an R like this, try to say an L sound but instead of making contact with the ridge that lies just above your teeth, brush past that ridge very quickly with the tip of your tongue. This is a lot easier in some positions than others; for example, it is usually much easier to pronounce a rolled R before a vowel than at the end of a word or before another consonant. In the second version of *R*, the tongue brushes past the roof of the mouth. This sound is surprisingly easy to produce, and for many English speakers, it may be easier to produce than a rolled R— though again, it is the version that may sound stranger to you. Essentially, say the letter L but do not make full contact with the roof of your mouth—try to brush past it with your tongue. As with *T* and *D*, the first version of *R* is the more common default version, while the second version is indicated by an *R* with a ot beneath it, as follows:

गाड़ी

gaaṛi

car

लड़का

laṛka

boy

तेरह

terah

thirteen

रात

raat

night

The letter *N* is also pronounced in two different ways. Usually, this letter is pronounced just as in English. However, at the end of a word, *N* can also indicate that any vowel that appears directly before it is "nasal". (Other resources will say that nasal *N*s also appear in other positions, but I personally can't hear the difference between non-final nasal *N*s and normal *N*s). Say any vowel sound as normal, but while you are saying it, breathe through your nostrils in addition to breathing through your mouth. Making a nasal sound like this should be easy, but as with many of these sounds, don't exaggerate them too much, or you will sound a little silly. In the system used in this book to represent Hindi sounds with English letters, those *N*s that denote a nasal sound have not been distinguished from the *N*s that are pronounced normally. This is because there was no elegant way of doing this that would not resort to the use of even more special marks; however, the main reason was that you will very soon become used to which words contain a "nasal" *N* since these words are some of the most common in the language. There are two main types of word in which a final *N* is prounced nasal. First, if any helper is directly added onto any other word, then any final *N* in that helper is nasal:

औरतें

auraten

women

वे बोलें गे

vo bolen ge

they will speak

Second, some very common words end with nasal *N*s; these words include *"mein"* – "I", *"men"* – "in", *"yahaan"* – "here", *"vahaan"* – "there", *"kahaan"* – "where?"*, and *"kyon?"* – "why?":

मैं बोलता था
mein bolta tha
I used to speak

कमरे में
kamre men
in the room

वह यहां है
vo yahaan hei
he is here

आप वहां क्यों जाते हैं?
Aap vahaan kyon jaate hein?
Why do you go there?

Finally, I said in Chapter One that the letter *V* was pronounced as in English. However, most Hindi speakers actually pronounce this letter as somewhere between the English pronunciation of V and the English pronunciation of W. Say a V sound now; your top row of teeth should be touching your bottom lip. To make the *V* sound in Hindi, make the same movement as you do for the English V but don't allow your teeth to touch your lip—your teeth should be very close to your lip, but not touching (again, this takes practice, but it is a simple enough movement when you know how). If you find this mixed V/W sound difficult to produce, use either version; either pronounce the letter *V* in Hindi as you do in English or pronounce it as you do the letter W. Of course, to Hindi ears, this letter is of course not pronounced in two different ways—it only sounds that way to English ears:

जवान
javaan
young ~or *"jawaan"*

जानवार
jaanvaar
animal ~or *"jaanwaar"*

Chapter Four: Words

This chapter contains a list of several hundred common words in Hindi; this list is divided into four sub-lists: objects, helpers, descriptors, and actions. Objects, helpers, and descriptors are further divided into groups of related words. This list is essentially a foundation; you should continue to add to it as you encounter new words (see the Conclusion for some suggestions about continuing to improve your Hindi after finishing this book). The first thing you may notice is the letters of some Hindi words have been underlined:

बिस्तर	bi_st_ar	bed
शब्दकोश	sha_bd_kosh	dictionary
इम्तहान	i_mt_ahaan	exam
दोस्त	do_st_	friend

The reason for this is connected with Hindi script and will be described in Chapter Six. For now, if you want to eventually learn Hindi script, it would be a good idea to remember whether the words you are learning contain underlined letters.

Some of the other symbols used in these lists may also need some explanation. The symbol ~ is used to clarify the meaning of a word, where a translation may otherwise be ambiguous:

ज़ुकाम	*zukaam*	cold ~illness
मुफ़्त	*muft*	free ~of charge

The symbol / shows there are multiple translations of the same word; it essentially means "or":

घर / मकान	*ghar / makaan*	house
यह	*ye*	he / she / it ~near

As mentioned in Chapter Two, some helpers make the objects they appear with act as though they were denoting more than one thing. These helpers always come after an object, and in the following list, they appear under the heading "Helpers that come after objects":

में	*men*	in
के साथ	*ke saath*	with

लड़के	लड़के के साथ
larke	*larke ke saath*
boys	with the boy

Likewise, in Hindi, some things that are not alive are actually referred to as though they were women. In the lists in this chapter, these objects have been listed under the heading "Objects referred to as if they were women":

किताब   kitaab   book

इमारत   imaarat   building

अच्छी किताब   आदमी की इमारत

acchi kitaab   *aadmi ki imaarat*

the good book   the man's building

Some animals are also spoken about as if they were women:

चिड़िया   ciṛiya   bird

बिल्ली   billi   cat

अच्छी चिड़िया   लड़के की बिल्ली

acchi ciṛiya   *laṛke ki billi*

the good bird   the boy's cat

Other grammar books will tell you that because of this fact, there are essentially two groups of objects in Hindi: those objects that are "feminine" and those that are "masculine". Many languages are described as having two or more groups of objects like this, and these groups are often referred to in terms of gender. (There are also languages, such as German, with a "neuter" group—and even languages with several different groups of objects). Personally, I do not think using gender labels is the best grammatical description for objects in Hindi (and many other languages) for two reasons. First, if you do use gender labels like this, English speakers will sometimes get confused because not only is this something that has no widespread equivalent in English (beyond calling a ship "she" for example). English learners often mix up rules—they use "masculine" rules with "feminine" objects because they themselves are males, for example, though by itself, this reason is not enough to justify the change in grammatical perspective I am proposing.

The second and more fundamental reason is that classifying all objects in Hindi as either "masculine" or "feminine" is incredibly inefficient. In my view, for Hindi, it is simply necessary to learn the "default" rules for objects and then learn the "special" rules for how to talk about women. (Another reason to avoid the "masculine" label is because these "default" rules are often the ones you use for talking about men, so using gender labels could even bring sexual politics into what should be a neutral grammatical situation). Once you have learned the rules for talking about women, it is then a simple step to think of examples in English of calling ships or cars or countries "she" and apply that same principle on a larger scale. The beauty of this approach is that the number of rules you subsequently have to learn about objects is thus dramatically reduced—and you can have fun (and so learn these "feminine nouns" more easily) referring to your elbow or your chair or your car as if they were girls.

Objects: Basic objects

हिसाबि	*hisaab*	account
पता	*pata*	address
जानवार	*jaan-vaar*	animal
जवाब	*javaab*	answer
सेब	*seb*	apple
केला	*kela*	banana
ग़ुसलख़ाना	*gusalkhaana*	bathroom
भालू	*bhaalu*	bear
बिस्तर	*bis̱tar*	bed
कंबल	*kanbal*	blanket
ख़ून	*khoon*	blood
शरीर	*shareer*	body
डिब्बा	*ḍibba*	box
लड़का	*laṛka*	boy
दिमाग़	*dimaag*	brain
पुल	*pul*	bridge
भाई	*bhai*	brother
मक्खन	*makkhan*	butter
ऊंट	*ooṇṭ*	camel
क़ालीन	*kaaleen*	carpet
पनीर	*paneer*	cheese
सीना	*seena*	chest
बच्चा	*bacca*	child
गिरजाघर	*gir-jaaghar*	church
शहर	*shahar*	city
बादल	*baadal*	cloud
ज़ुकाम	*zukaam*	cold ~illness
रंग	*rang*	colour
रसोइया	*rasoiya*	cook

देश	*desh*	country
प्याला	*pyaala*	cup
परदा	*par-da*	curtain
तकिया	*takiya*	cushion
बाप	*baap*	dad
बेटी	*beṭi*	daughter
दिन	*din*	day
शब्दकोश	*sha<u>bd</u>kosh*	dictionary
डाकटर	*ḍaakṭar*	doctor
कुत्ता	*kutta*	dog
दरवाजा	*dar-vaaza*	door
कान	*kaan*	ear
अंडा	*anḍa*	egg
हाथी	*haathi*	elephant
इम्तहान	*im<u>t</u>ahaan*	exam
उदाहरण	*udaaharan*	example
मुख	*mukh*	face
मेला	*mela*	fair
परिवार	*parivaar*	family
पंखा	*pankha*	fan
किसान	*kisaan*	farmer
पिता	*pita*	father
फूल	*phool*	flower
खाना	*khaana*	food
पैर	*peir*	foot
माथा	*maatha*	forehead
वन	*van*	forest
दोस्त	*dos<u>t</u>*	friend
सामान	*saamaan*	furniture
लहसुन	*lahsun*	garlic
लड़की	*laṛki*	girl

गिलास	gilaas	glass ~tumbler
अंगूर	angoor	grape
मेहमान	mahmaan	guest
बाल	baal	hair
हाथ	haath	hand
सुख	sukh	happiness
सिर	sir	head
दिल	dil	heart
छेद	ched	hole
घर	ghar	home
शहद	shahad	honey
घोड़ा	ghoṛa	horse
होटल	hoṭal	hotel
घंटा	ghaṇṭa	hour
घर / मकान	ghar / makaan	house
पति	pati	husband
विचार	vicaar	idea
जेल	jel	jail
सफ़र	safar	journey
जज	jaj	judge
रस	ras	juice
चाकू	caaku	knife
चमड़ा	camṛa	leather
नींबू	ninbu	lemon
ख़त	khat	letter ~post
झूठ	jhooṭh	lie
शेर	sher	lion
प्यार	pyaar	love
आदमी	aadmi	man
आम	aam	mango
ढंग	ḍhang	manner

नक्शा	naksha	map
बाज़ार	baazaar	market
गोश्त	gosht	meat
संदेश	sandesh	message
दूध	doodh	milk
शीशा	sheesha	mirror
पैसा	peisa	money
बंदर	bandar	monkey
महीना	maheena	month
चांद	caand	moon
माता	maata	mother
चूहा	cooha	mouse
मुंह	munh	mouth
मां	maan	mum
संगीत	sangeet	music
नाम	naam	name
अख़बार	akhbaar	newspaper
दफ्तर	daftar	office
तेल	tel	oil
प्याज	pyaaz	onion
दर्द	dard	pain
महल	mahal	palace
काग़ज़	kaagaz	paper
मटर	matar	pea
आड़ू	aaru	peach
क़लम	kalam	pen
लोग	log	people
व्यक्ति	vyakti	person
आलू	aalu	potato
दाम	daam	price
सवाल	savaal	question

ख़रगोश	*khar-gosh*	rabbit
कारण	*kaaran*	reason
धर्म	*dharm*	religion
जवाब	*javaab*	reply
चावल	*caaval*	rice
कमरा	*kam-ra*	room
नमक	*namak*	salt
बालू	*baalu*	sand
स्कूल	*skool*	school
समुद्र	*samudr*	sea
नौकर	*naukar*	servant
जहाज़	*jahaaz*	ship
जूता	*joota*	shoe
दुकानदार	*dukaan-daar*	shopkeeper
रेशम	*resham*	silk
बहिन	*bahin*	sister
आकाश	*aakaash*	sky
सांप	*saanp*	snake
साबुन	*saabun*	soap
सैनिक	*seinik*	soldier
बेटा	*beṭa*	son
गाना	*gaana*	song
मसाला	*masaala*	spice
चम्मच	*cammac*	spoon
चौक	*cauk*	square ~place
तूफ़ान	*toofaan*	storm
विद्यार्थी	*vidyaarthi*	student
सूरज	*sooraj*	sun
अंगूठा	*angootha*	thumb
टिकट	*ṭikaṭ*	ticket
समय	*samay*	time

टमाटर	*ṭamaaṭar*	tomato
दांत	*daant*	tooth
शहर	*shahar*	town
पैंट	*peinṭ*	trousers
गांव	*gaanv*	village
पानी	*paani*	water
मौसम	*mausam*	weather
हफ़्ता	*haf̱ta*	week
पत्नी	*pat̲ni*	wife
औरत	*aurat*	woman
शब्द	*shab̲d*	word
काम	*kaam*	work
साल	*saal*	year

Objects referred to as if they were women

उम्र	*umr*	age ~of a person
हवा	*hava*	air
सेना	*sena*	army
पीठ	*peeṭh*	back
दाढ़ी	*daaṛhi*	beard
चिड़िया	*ciṛiya*	bird
नाव	*naav*	boat
किताब	*kitaab*	book
बोतल	*botal*	bottle
रोटी	*roṭi*	bread
इमारत	*imaarat*	building
बस	*bas*	bus
गोभी	*gobhi*	cabbage
गाड़ी	*gaaṛi*	car

गाजर	*gaajar*	carrot
बिल्ली	*billi*	cat
कुर्सी	*kursi*	chair
मुर्गी	*murgi*	chicken
मलाई	*malai*	cream
पोशाक	*poshaak*	dress
कुहनी	*kuhni*	elbow
आंख	*aankh*	eye
फ़ीस	*fees*	fee
उंगली	*ungli*	finger
आग	*aag*	fire
मछली	*machli*	fish
सरकार	*sar-kaar*	government
छुट्टी	*chuṭṭi*	holiday
नौकरी	*naukari*	job ~employment
चाबी	*caabi*	key
रसोइ	*rasoi*	kitchen
झील	*jheel*	lake
भाषा	*bhaasha*	language
टंग	*ṭang*	leg
ज़िंदगी	*zindagi*	life
बत्ती	*batti*	light ~lamp
दवा	*dava*	medicine ~drugs
मीटिंग	*meeṭing*	meeting
ग़लती	*galti*	mistake
सुबह	*subah*	morning
मसजिद	*masjid*	mosque
गरदन	*gar-dan*	neck
ख़बर	*khabar*	news
रात	*raat*	night
नाक	*naak*	nose

नाशपाती	naashpaati	pear
इजाज़त	ijaazat	permission
तस्वीर	tasveer	picture
जगह	jagah	place
जेब	jeb	pocket
बारिश	baarish	rain
सड़क	saṛak	road
छत	chat	roof
कैंची	keinci	scissors
सेवा	seva	service
क़मीज़	kameez	shirt
दुकान	dukaan	shop
बग़ल	bagal	side
चमड़ी	camṛi	skin
बर्फ़	barf	snow
कहानी	kahaani	story
चीनी	ceeni	sugar
धूप	dhoop	sunshine
मिठाई	miṭhai	sweets
मेज़	mez	table
चाय	caay	tea
चीज़	ceez	thing
जीभ	jeebh	tongue
मीनार	meenaar	tower
थाली	thaali	tray
आवाज़	aavaaz	voice
दीवार	deevaar	wall
हवा	hava	wind
खिड़की	khiṛki	window
दुनिया	duniya	world
कलाई	kalai	wrist

हिंदी	*Hindi*	Hindi
अंग्रेज़ी	*Angrezi*	English
उर्दू	*Urdu*	Urdu
संस्कृत	*San<u>s</u>krit*	Sanskrit

"he", "she", "it"

वह	*vo*	he / she / it ~distant
वे	*vo*	they ~distant
यह	*ye*	he / she / it ~near
ये	*ye*	they ~near
मैं	*mein*	I
हम	*ham*	we
तू	*tu*	you ~one person
तुम	*tum*	you ~more than one
आप	*aap*	you ~polite

"this", "these", "that"

यह	*ye*	this
ये	*ye*	these
वह	*vo*	that
वे	*vo*	those

Objects used in questions

कैसे	keise	how?
क्या	kya	what?
कब	kab	when?
कहां	kahaan	where?
कौन	kaun	who?
क्यों	kyon	why?

"anybody", "somebody", "nothing"

कोई	koi	anyone
कुछ भी	kuch bhi	anything
दोनों	donon	both
सब कुछ	sab kuch	everything
सब लोग	sab log	everyone
और	aur	more
कुछ नहीं	kuch naheen	nothing
कोई नहीं	koi naheen	no one
कोई भी नहीं	koi bhi naheen	no one at all
कुछ भी नहिं	kuch bhi naheen	nothing at all
कुछ	kuch	something
कोई	koi	someone
कुछ	kuch	some

Objects denoting when something happens

फिर से / दोबारह	*phir se / dobaarah*	again
रात भर	*raat bhar*	all night
हमेशा	*hamesha*	always
कभी	*kabhi*	ever
पहले	*pahle*	first
कभी नहीं	*kabhi naheen*	never
अब	*ab*	now
कभी कभी	*kabhi kabhi*	now and then
अक्सर	*ak̲sar*	often
पहले	*pahle*	previously
फिर	*phir*	then ~after that
आज	*aaj*	today
कल	*kal*	tomorrow
कल	*kal*	yesterday

Objects denoting where something happens

ऊपर	*oopar*	above
आगे	*aage*	ahead
पीछे	*peeche*	back
पीछे	*peeche*	behind
नीचे	*neece*	below
दूर	*door*	far
आगे	*aage*	forward
यहां	*yahaan*	here
इधर	*idhar*	here ~to here
कहीं कहीं	*kaheen kaheen*	here and there
इधर उधर	*idhar udhar*	here and there
अंदर	*andar*	in

सामने	saamne	in front
अंदर	andar	inside
पास में	paas men	nearby
रास्ते में	raaste men	on the way
सामने	saamne	opposite
बाहर	baahar	out
बाहर	baahar	outside
ऊपर	oopar	over
यहीं	yaheen	right here
वहीं	vaheen	right there
कहीं	kaheen	somewhere
वहां	vahaan	there
उधर	udhar	there ~to there
ऊपर	oopar	up
किधर	kidhar	where? ~to where

Objects denoting how something happens

ज़रूर	zaroor	certainly
ज़ोर से	zor se	forcefully
ख़ुशी से	khushi se	gladly
शायद	shaayad	maybe
शायद	shaayad	perhaps
आहिस्ता	aahista	slowly
ऐसे	eise	this way
वैसे	veise	this way

Countries, cities, languages

बहरीन	*Bah-reen*	Bahrain
ब्राज़िल	*Braazil*	Brazil
ब्रिटेन	*Briṭen*	Britain
कनाडा	*Kanaaḍa*	Canada
चीन	*Ceen*	China
इंगलैंड	*Ingleinḍ*	England
भारत	*Bhaarat*	India
ईरान	*Eeraan*	Iran
इराक	*Iraak*	Iraq
जापान	*Jaapaan*	Japan
कुवैत	*Kuveit*	Kuwait
पाकिस्तान	*Paaki<u>s</u>taan*	Pakistan
पोलैंड	*Poleinḍ*	Poland
रूस	*Roos*	Russia
स्पेन	*Spen*	Spain
सीरिया	*Seeriya*	Syria
टर्की	*Ṭurki*	Turkey
अफ्रीका	*Afreeka*	Africa
अमेरिका	*Amerika*	America
एशिया	*Eshiya*	Asia
यूरोप	*Yoorop*	Europe
दिल्ली	*Dilli*	Delhi
मुम्बई	*Mu<u>m</u>bai*	Mumbai
चेन्नई	*Cennai*	Chennai
लंदन	*Landan*	London
न्यू यार्क	*Nyu Yaark*	New York

Days of the week

सोमवार	*Somvaar*	Monday
मंगलवार	*Mangalvaar*	Tuesday
बुधवार	*Budhavaar*	Wednesday
गुरुवार	*Guruvaar*	Thursday
शुक्रवार	*Shukravaar*	Friday
शनिवार	*Shanivaar*	Saturday
रविवार	*Ravivaar*	Sunday

Helpers: Helpers used before objects

कुछ	kuch	a few
बहुत	bahut	a lot
कुछ	kuch	any
और	aur	more
कोई	koi	no
काफ़ी	kaafi	plenty of
कई	kai	several
कुछ	kuch	some
कोई	koi	some ~several
कुछ और	kuch aur	some more
कोई और	koi aur	some other
वह	vo	that
ये	ye	these
यह	ye	this
वे	vo	those
क्या	kya	what!
क्या	kya	what?

Helpers used after objects

के ऊपर	ke oopar	above
पर	par	at
के पीछे	ke peeche	behind
तक	tak	by ~a time
से	se	by ~by means of
के लिए	ke lie	for
से	se	for ~duration
से	se	from

में	*men*	in
की जगह	*ki jagah*	in place of
में	*men*	into
पर	*par*	on
को	*ko*	on ~a day or date
को	*ko*	to
की तरफ़	*ki taraf*	toward
तक	*tak*	until
के साथ	*ke saath*	with

Helpers used before descriptors

और भी	*aur bhi*	even more
ज़्यादा	*zyaada*	more
और	*aur*	more
काफ़ी	*kaafi*	quite
कुछ कुछ	*kuch kuch*	somewhat
बहुत	*bahut*	very

Helpers used before whole phrases

क्योंकि	*kyonki*	because
अगर	*agar*	if
कि	*ki*	that
इसलिए	*islie*	therefore
जब	*jab*	when

Helpers used as in English

नमस्ते	*nama<u>st</u>e*	hello
जी हां	*ji haan*	yes
जी नहीं	*ji naheen*	no
शायद	*shaayad*	perhaps
धन्यवाद	*dhanyavaad*	thank you
और	*aur*	and
या	*ya*	or
लेकिन	*lekin*	but

Descriptors: Basic descriptors

अकेला	*akela*	alone
बुरा	*bura*	bad
सुंदर	*sundar*	beautiful
बड़ा	*baṛa*	big
सस्ता	*sa<u>s</u>ta*	cheap
साफ़	*saaf*	clean
ठंडा	*ṭhanḍa*	cold
ख़तरनाक	*khatar-naak*	dangerous
अंधेरा	*andhera*	dark
गहरा	*gah-ra*	deep
मुश्किल	*mu<u>sh</u>kil*	difficult
मैला	*meila*	dirty
आसान	*aasaan*	easy
ख़ाली	*khaali*	empty
अंग्रेज़ी	*Angrezi*	English
मोटा	*moṭa*	fat
विदेशी	*videshi*	foreign
मुफ़्त	*mu<u>ft</u>*	free ~of charge
मिलनसार	*milan-saar*	friendly
अच्छा	*accha*	good
भारी	*bhaari*	heavy
ईमानदार	*eemaan-daar*	honest
गर्म	*garm*	hot
बीमार	*beemaar*	ill
अहम	*aḥam*	important
होशियार	*hoshiyaar*	intelligent
आलसी	*aalsi*	lazy
लंबा	*lanba*	long
अगला	*agla*	next

बूढ़ा	*booṛha*	old ~for people
पुराना	*puraana*	old ~for things
ग़रीब	*gareeb*	poor
मुमकिन	*mumkin*	possible
तैयार	*teiyaar*	ready
अमीर	*ameer*	rich
ठीक	*ṭheek*	right ~correct
उदास	*udaas*	sad
धीमा	*dheema*	slow
छोटा	*choṭa*	small
नरम	*naram*	soft
विशेष	*vishesh*	special
अजीब	*ajeeb*	strange
मीठा	*meeṭha*	sweet
लंबा	*lanba*	tall ~for people
पतला	*patla*	thin
सच	*sac*	true
कमज़ोर	*kamzor*	weak
गीला	*geela*	wet
जवान	*javaan*	young

Colours

काला	*kaala*	black
नीला	*neela*	blue
भूरा	*bhoora*	brown
हरा	*hara*	green
लाल	*laal*	red
सफ़ेद	*safed*	white
पीला	*peela*	yellow

Unique numbers

एक	*ek*	1
दो	*do*	2
तीन	*teen*	3
चार	*caar*	4
पांच	*paanc*	5
छह	*chah*	6
सात	*saat*	7
आठ	*aaṭh*	8
नौ	*nau*	9
दस	*das*	10
ग्यारह	*gyaarah*	11
बारह	*baarah*	12
तेरह	*terah*	13
चौदह	*caudah*	14
पंद्रह	*pandrah*	15
सोलह	*solah*	16
सत्रह	*satrah*	17
अठारह	*aṭhaarah*	18
उन्नीस	*unnees*	19
बीस	*bees*	20
इक्कीस	*ikkees*	21
बाईस	*baees*	22
तेईस	*te-ees*	23
चौबीस	*caubees*	24
पच्चीस	*paccees*	25
छब्बीस	*chabbees*	26
सत्ताईस	*sattaees*	27
अट्ठाईस	*aṭṭhaees*	28
उनतीस	*untees*	29

तीस	*tees*	30
इकत्तीस	*ikattees*	31
बत्तीस	*battees*	32
तैंतीस	*teintees*	33
चौंतीस	*cauntees*	34
पैंतीस	*peintees*	35
छत्तीस	*chattees*	36
सैंतीस	*seintees*	37
अड़तीस	*aṛtees*	38
उनतालीस	*untaalees*	39
चालीस	*caalees*	40
इकतालीस	*iktaalees*	41
बयालीस	*bayaalees*	42
तैंतालीस	*teintaalees*	43
चवालीस	*cavaalees*	44
पैंतालीस	*peintaalees*	45
छियालीस	*chiyaalees*	46
सैंतालीस	*seintaalees*	47
अड़तालीस	*aṛtaalees*	48
उनचास	*un-caas*	49
पचास	*pacaas*	50
इक्यावन	*ikyaavan*	51
बावन	*baavan*	52
तिरपन	*tir-pan*	53
चौवन	*cauvan*	54
पचपन	*pacpan*	55
छप्पन	*chappan*	56
सत्तावन	*sattaavan*	57
अट्ठावन	*aṭṭhaavan*	58
उनसठ	*unsaaṭh*	59
साठ	*saaṭh*	60

इकसठ	*iksaṭh*	61
बासठ	*baasaṭh*	62
तिरसठ	*tir-saṭh*	63
चौंसठ	*caunsaṭh*	64
पैंसठ	*peinsaṭh*	65
छियासठ	*chiyaasaṭh*	66
सरसठ	*sar-saṭh*	67
अड़सठ	*aṛsaṭh*	68
उनहत्तर	*un-hattar*	69
सत्तर	*sattar*	70
इकहत्तर	*ik-hattar*	71
बहत्तर	*bahattar*	72
तिहत्तर	*tihattar*	73
चौहत्तर	*cauhattar*	74
पचहत्तर	*pac-hattar*	75
छिहत्तर	*chihattar*	76
सतहत्तर	*sat-hattar*	77
अठहत्तर	*aṭh-hattar*	78
उन्यसी	*unyaasi*	79
अस्सी	*assi*	80
इक्यासी	*ikyaasi*	81
बयासी	*bayaasi*	82
तिरासी	*tiraasi*	83
चौरासी	*cauraasi*	84
पचासी	*pacaasi*	85
छियासी	*chiyaasi*	86
सत्तासी	*sattaasi*	87
अट्ठासी	*aṭṭhaasi*	88
नवासी	*navaasi*	89
नब्बे	*nabbe*	90
इक्यानवे	*ikyaan-ve*	91

बानवे	*baan-ve*	92
तिरानवे	*tiraan-ve*	93
चौरानवे	*cauraan-ve*	94
पचानवे	*pacaan-ve*	95
छियानवे	*chiyaan-ve*	96
सत्तानवे	*sattaan-ve*	97
अट्ठानवे	*aṭṭhaan-ve*	98
निंयानवे	*ninyaan-ve*	99
सौ	*sau*	100
हज़ार	*hazaar*	1000
पहले	*pahla*	first
दूसरा	*doos-ra*	second
तीसरा	*tees-ra*	third
चौथा	*cautha*	fourth
छठा	*chaṭa*	sixth
नवां	*navaan*	ninth

Other descriptors

कितना	*kitna*	how much?
इतना	*itna*	so much
उतना	*utna*	so much
ऐसा	*eisa*	such
वैसा	*veisa*	such
जैसा	*jeisa*	such as
उतना	*utna*	that much
इतना	*itna*	this much
कौन सा	*kaun sa*	which?

Actions: Basic actions

पूछ	*pooch*	ask
बन	*ban*	become
तोड़	*toṛ*	break
ला	*la*	bring
बना	*bana*	build
ख़रीद	*khareed*	buy
पकड़	*pakaṛ*	catch
चुन	*cun*	choose
आ	*a*	come
पका	*paka*	cook
रो	*ro*	cry
नाच	*naac*	dance
मर	*mar*	die
कर	*kar*	do
पी	*pi*	drink
चला	*cala*	drive
खा	*kha*	eat
लड़	*laṛ*	fight
पा	*pa*	find
भूल	*bhool*	forget
दे	*de*	give
जा	*ja*	go
सुन	*sun*	hear
मार	*maar*	hit
जान	*jaan*	know
हंस	*hans*	laugh
बना	*bana*	make
मिल	*mil*	meet
खेल	*khel*	play

पढ़	paṛh	read
कह	kah	say
देख	dekh	see
लग	lag	seem
बेच	bec	sell
भेज	bhej	send
गा	ga	sing
बैठ	beiṭh	sit
सो	so	sleep
मुस्करा	mus<u>k</u>ara	smile
बोल	bol	speak
रह	rah	stay
चुरा	cura	steal
रोक	rok	stop
पढ़	paṛh	study
तैर	teir	swim
ले	le	take
बता	bata	tell
सोच	soc	think
फेंक	phenk	throw
समझ	samajh	understand
चल	cal	walk
चाह	caah	want
धो	dho	wash
पहन	pahn	wear
जीत	jeet	win
लिख	likh	write

Chapter Five: Elevations

An elevation is a mental tool for learning complex rules in languages. It is designed to categorise a phrase that has an *actual* meaning that is different from its *literal* translation, the literal translation being analysed in terms of rules that are purposefully simpler than the rules that would otherwise be needed to analyse that phrase—now, this sounds very complicated However, the concept really isn't that difficult once you get used to it. Let's start by considering an example:

mujhe kitaab pasand hei

According to the rules described so far, the literal translation of this phrase is something like "to me the book *'pasand'* is". Clearly, this doesn't make much sense, and not just because we do not know what the word "*pasand*" means. Yet, however strange such a translation might appear, it is crucial to note that the rules we have learned so far do allow us to give the phrase this literal translation:

mujhe kitaab pasand hei > to me the book "*pasand*" is

This phrase does in fact have an actual meaning in Hindi; this meaning is "I like the book". The literal translation is *elevated* to denote the actual meaning: "I like the book":

I like this book
mujhe kitaab pasand hei > ~~to me the book "pasand" is~~

We could of course create an explicit rule to describe this, such as "to denote the verb 'like', an experiencer subject is used, which is expressed by a pronoun in the dative case occuring before a semantic object that acts as the grammatical subject; the predicate adjective '*pasand*' is used with the copular verb, and the semantic subject thus syntactically functions as an adjunct…". Evidently, this is not the easiest way to learn how to say "I like the book" in Hindi! (I have even seen resources written for English-speaking learners of foreign languages that seem to focus on teaching those learners about English grammar!)   Instead of studying for a degree in linguistics before we can learn how to say "I like the book", we can just remember this single example:

मुझे किताब पसंद है
mujhe kitaab pasand hei
I like the book

The key is the literal translation we were able to give the phrase earlier; you simply use the rules you have learned so far in this book to modify the literal translation in order to express a desired actual meaning.

The fact that in this example, you may not know what *"pasand"* means has absolutely no bearing; you just need to recognise (from how it is used in the phrase) that it is a descriptor:

तुझे किताब पसंद है
tujhe kitaab pasand hei
you like the book

हमें क़ालीन पसंद था
hamen kaaleen pasand tha
we liked the carpet

The crucial advantage of doing this of course is that the rules we are using are all relatively simple, especially in comparison to the ones we would otherwise have to learn (see above)—or the rules that other grammar resources expect learners to understand. I am sure that learning a whole new "language" of grammatical terminology is not why you started to learn Hindi, and there is absolutely no need for the convoluted linguistic rules you will encounter in many other grammar books. Like the other grammatical "tools" presented in this book, elevations can be used when learning any language; they both reduce the actual number of rules you have to learn and ensure you will never again have to learn convoluted rules for the more complex structures of the language you are learning. The remainder of this chapter is essentially a list of example elevations for you to learn; as in Chapter Four, this list is by no means exhaustive. Although I have given a basic explanation of each elevation, you should study primarily the example itself. Look for the underlying literal structure and apply the simple rules you have learned.

"have"

Unlike in English, there is no action in Hindi that denotes "have", as in "the man has a pen", "I had a book", etc. In Hindi, you have to use a phrase with the helper "*ke paas*":

आदमी के पास एक क़लम है

aadmi ke paas ek kalam hei

the man has a pen

मेरी पास एक किताब थी

meri paas ek kitaab thi

I had a book

Note that this elevation is only used when the object possessed is a physical thing—and the possession is therefore temporary. When the object possessed is more abstract, as in "he has a cold", "he has a lot of work", etc, the helper "*ko*" is used:

आदमी को ज़ुकाम है

aadmi ko zukaam hei

the man has a cold

मुझे बहुत काम हो गा

mujhe bahut kaam ho ga

I will have a lot of work

When the possessed object is something that is a permanent possession, as in "he has a brother", "I have blue eyes", etc, the helper "*ka*" is used:

आदमी की बहिन है

aadmi ki bahin hei

the man has a sister

मेरी नीली आंखें हैं

meri neeli aankhen hein

I have blue eyes

"wants to speak"

To say "wants to speak", use the helper "...*na*" and the action "*caah*" – "want", as follows:

आदमी बोलना चाहता है
aadmi bolna caahta hei
the man wants to speak

मैं जाना चाहता हूं
mein jaana caahta hoon
I want to go

(Other authors will tell you that an action with this helper "...*na*" added to it is in fact something called an "infinitive", though of course, they won't use the labels "action" or "helper". In my view, this is misguided for Hindi because these authors then often *start* with the combined "infinitive" form as a basic unit; then, they delete the "...*na*" to form actions. In my view, this is very inefficient. I have read page after page of needless rules—for various languages—about how "infinitives", "present stems", and "imperfect stems" etc are formed. The pressure to conform to traditional grammatical conventions is so strong that the "infinitive" becomes the starting point for learning "verbs" when it should not be considered a separate category at all—and the learner has to subsequently learn and apply acrobatic rules about how to form the "verb stem". In my view, the most efficient way of learning what in other books may be called the "verb stem" is by simply learning the "verb stem" itself as the actual action! To me, the "infinitive" is best learned as an instance of a specific helper added to an action. When you are using resources to continue to improve your Hindi, be very careful when you read about anything called an "infinitive".)

"must speak"

To say "must speak", use the helper "*...na*" and the action "*parr*", as follows:

आदमी को बोलना पड़े गा
aadmi ko bolna paṛe ga
the man must speak

मुझे जाना पड़े गा
mujhe jaana paṛe ga
I must go

To say "has to speak" (in the sense of "needs to speak"), use the helper "*...na*" as follows:

आदमी को बोलना है
aadmi ko bolna hei
the man has to speak

मुझे जाना था
mujhe jaana tha
I had to go

"should speak"

To say "should see", use the helper "*...na*" and the descriptor "*caahie*", as follows:

आदमी को बोलना चाहिए
aadmi ko bolna caahie
the man should speak

इसे जाना चाहिए
ise jaana caahie
he should go

"can speak"

To say "can speak" or "is able to see", use the action "*sak*" with another action, as follows:

आदमी बोल सकता है
*aadmi bol **sak**ta hei*
the man can speak

मैं जा सका
*mein ja **saka***
I was able to go

"is speaking"

Likewise, to say "is speaking", use the action "*rah*" with another action, as follows:

आदमी बोल रहा है
*aadmi bol **raha** hei*
the man is speaking

औरत जा रही थी
*aurat ja **rahi** thi*
the woman was going

In this instance, the helper "...*a*" does not become "...*een*":

आदमी बोल रहे थे
aadmi bol rahe the
the men were speaking

औरतें बोल रही थीं
auraten bol rahi theen
the women were speaking

(Note that this is different from English, in which "is", "was", or "will be" is used with a descriptor such as "seeing", "eating", or "going" etc; in English, there is no structural difference between phrases like "he is seeing", "he is seen", or "he is happy".)

To say "is going to speak", just say "will speak":

आदमी बोले गा

aadmi bole ga

the man will speak

आदमी बोले गा

aadmi bole ga

the man is going to speak

"has already spoken"

To say "has already spoken", use the action "*cuk*" with another action, as follows:

आदमी बोल चुका है

*aadmi bol **cuka** hei*

the man has already spoken

औरत जा चुकी थी

*aurat ja **cuki** thi*

the woman had already gone

"Does he speak?"

To ask a question, simply use the helper "*kya*" before a whole phrase—do not reverse the order of the words as in English:

आदमी बोलता है

aadmi bolta hei

the man speaks

क्या आदमी बोलता है

***Kya** aadmi bolta hei?*

Does the man speak?

"might speak"

To say "might speak", use the helper "...e" by, and a itself (not in combination with "ga") and add the helper "shaayad", as follows:

आदमी शायद बोले
aadmi **shaayad** *bole*
the man might speak

आदमी शायद बोलें
aadmi **shaayad** *bolen*
the men might speak

मैं शायद बोलूं
mein **shaayad** *boloon*
I might speak

तुम शायद बोलो
tum **shaayad** *bolo*
you might speak

Remember that with the helper "...e", the final *E* of "de" and "le" is dropped:

आदमी शायद दे
aadmi shaayad de
the man might give

आदमी शायद दें
aadmi shaayad den
the men might give

आदमी शायद ले
aadmi shaayad le
the man might take

आदमी शायद लें
aadmi shaayad len
the men might take

मैं शायद दूं
mein shaayad doon
I might give

तुम शायद लो
tum shaayad lo
you might take

To say "might be", the helper "*hei*" becomes "*ho*"—forms for "*mein*" and "*tum*" do not change:

आदमी शायद अच्छा हो
*aadmi shaayad accha **ho***
the man might be good

आदमी शायद अच्छे हों
*aadmi shaayad acche **hon***
the men might be good

मैं शायद अच्छा हूं
mein shaayad accha hoon
I might be good

तुम शायद अच्छे हो
tum shaayad acche ho
you might be good

"does not speak"

To say "the man does not speak" etc, put the helper "*naheen*" directly before any action:

आदमी नहीं बोलता है
*aadmi **naheen** bolta hei*
the man does not speak

आदमी नहीं बोलता था
*aadmi **naheen** bolta tha*
the man did not use to speak

आदमी नहीं बोला
*aadmi **naheen** bola*
the man did not speak

वह शायद नहीं बोले
*vo shaayad **naheen** bole*
he might not speak

वह नहीं बोला है
*vo **naheen** bola hei*
he has not spoken

वह शायद अच्छा नहीं हो
*vo shaayad accha **naheen** ho*
he might not be good

"is spoken"

To say "is spoken", you essentially say "it spoke goes", as follows:

वह बला जाता है
vo bola jaata hei
it is spoken

औरत देखी गयी
aurat dekhi gayi
the woman was seen

वह खाया जाता है
vo khaaya jaata hei
it is eaten

आदमी देखे गए
aadmi dekhe gaye
the men were seen

"the man who"

As mentioned in Chapter Three, to say "the man who", the object "*jo*" is used to refer to a previous object, as follows:

वह आदमी जो कल आया
*vo aadmi **jo** kal aaya*
the man who came yesterday

वह आदमी जिसे मैं किताब देता हूं
*vo aadmi **jise** mein kitaab deta hoon*
the man to whom I give the book

"this book", "that book", "these book?"

The objects *"ye"*, *"vo"*, and *"kya"* may also function as helpers; they can appear before objects to denote the following:

यह किताब
ye *kitaab*
this book

वह किताब
vo *kitaab*
that book

ये किताबें
ye *kitaaben*
these books

वे किताबें
vo *kitaaben*
those books

क्या किताब
kya *kitaab?*
what book?

These helpers change exactly like their equivalent objects:

इस आदमी के लिए
is *aadmi ke lie*
for this man

उस लड़के से
us *larke se*
from that boy

उन किताबों में
un *kitaabon men*
in those books

किस किताब के लिए
kis *kitaab ke lie?*
for what book?

"him", "them", "me", "us"

As described in Chapter Three, the helper "ko" denotes "to" and appears after an object:

आदमी को

aadmi ko

to the man

औरत को

aurat ko

to the woman

However, this helper also appears after any object that is affected by an action—in a phrase like "he sees the woman" for example, the object that is affected by the action is "woman" because it is the thing that is being seen:

वह औरत को देखता है

vo aurat ko dekhta hei

he sees the woman

आदमी लड़के को देखता है

aadmi larke ko dekhta hei

the man sees the boy

However, if "*a woman*" is specifically denoted, the helper "ko" is not usually used:

वह एक औरत देखता है

vo ek aurat dekhta hei

he sees **a** woman

आदमी ने एक लड़का देखा

aadmi ne ek larka dekha

the man saw **a** boy

Because it is not possible to say "a" with objects such as *"ye"*, *"mein"*, or *"tu"* etc, these objects usually appear with *"ko"*. Therefore, words like "him", "them", "me", "us", etc can usually be translated as follows:

वह मुझे देखता है
vo mujhe dekhta hei
he sees **me**

वह हमें देखता है
vo hamen dekhta hei
he sees **us**

हम इसे देखते हैं
ham ise dekhte hein
we see **him**

हम इन्हें देखते हैं
ham inhen dekhte hein
we see **them**

वह तुझे देखता है
vo tujhe dekhta hei
he sees **you**

वह तुम्हें देखता है
vo tumhen dekhta hei
he sees **you**

Finally, note that if the object does not denote a human being, only use *"ko"* when you want to say phrases like "this book" or "that man", etc:

आदमी किताब देखता है
aadmi kitaab dekhta hei
the man sees the book

आदमी एक किताब देखता है
aadmi ek kitaab dekhta hei
the man sees a book

वह इस किताब को देखता है
vo is kitaab ko dekhta hei
he sees **this** book

वह उन किताबों को देखता है
vo un kitaabon ko dekhta hei
he sees **those** books

"himself", "myself", "yourself"

To say "himself", "myself", "yourself", etc, use the helper "*khud*" after an object, as follows:

आदमी ख़ुद गया

*aadmi **khud** gaya*
the man himself went

वह ख़ुद गया

*vo **khud** gaya*
he himself went

"both", "either", "neither"

These words are denoted by the helpers "*bhi*", "*ya*", and "*na*", and "*aur*", as follows:

वह किताब भी देखता है और क़लम भी

*vo kitaab **bhi** dekhta hei aur kalam **bhi***
he sees both the book and the pen

वह या किताब देखता है या क़लम

*vo **ya** kitaab dekhta hei **ya** kalam*
he sees either the book or the pen

वह न किताब देखता है न क़लम

*vo **na** kitaab dekhta hei **na** kalam*
he sees neither the book nor the pen

"my own"

As described in Chapter Three, the helper *"ka"* appears between two objects to denote that the second object belongs to the first—it also combines with the objects *"mein"*, *"ham"*, *"tu"* and *"tum"* to create special forms:

आदमी का सेब
*aadmi **ka** seb*
the man's apple

इसका सेब
*is **ka** seb*
his apple

मेरा सेब
***mera** seb*
my apple

हमारा सेब
***hamaara** seb*
our apple

तेरा सेब
***tera** seb*
your apple

तुम्हारा सेब
***tumhaara** seb*
your apple

However, the helper *"ka"* is not used when the person who owns the object is also the person who is performing an action; in this instance, the descriptor *"apna"* is used. This sounds complicated, so take a look at the following examples; in these examples, using *"ka"* would be impossible:

मैं अपना सेब खाता हूं
*mein **apna** seb khaata hoon*
I eat my apple ~not *"mein **mera** seb khaata hoon"*

तू अपनी किताब पढ़ता है
*tu **apni** kitaab paṛhta hei*
you read your book ~not "*tu **teri** kitaab paṛhta hei*

Logically, both alternatives are of course possible when talking about someone else:

आदमी अपना सेब खाता है
aadmi apna seb khaata hei
the man eats his apple ~his own apple

आदमी उसका सेब खाता है
aadmi us ka seb khaata hei
the man eats his apple ~someone else's apple

"if he speaks"

For phrases with the helper "*agar*" – "if", observe the following changes to actions; note also the use of the helper "*to*", which appears between two phrases:

अगर वह बोलता है तो मैं बोलूं गा
*agar vo bolta hei **to** mein boloon ga*
if he speaks, I will speak

अगर वह बोले तो मैं बोलूं
agar vo bole to mein boloon
if he spoke, I would speak

अगर वह बोलता तो मैं बोलता
agar vo bolta to mein bolta
if he had spoken, I would have spoken

"younger", "youngest"

Descriptors can be used to compare objects; you can say "younger" instead of "young", "bigger" instead of "big", "more beautiful" instead of "beautiful", etc. Likewise, you can say "youngest", "biggest", "most beautiful", etc. To do this in Hindi, simply use the following elevations:

आदमी औरत से जवान है
aadmi aurat se javaan hei
the man is younger than the woman

आदमी सब से जवान है
aadmi sab se javaan hei
the man is the youngest

Giving instructions

In order to tell someone to do something, use an action with the helper "*...e*":

(तुम) बोलो
(tum) bolo
speak

(आप) बोलें
(aap) bolen
speak

With "*tu*", just use the action by itself:

(तू) बोल
(tu) bol
speak

An alternative for "*aap*" is to use the helper "*...ie*", which never changes form:

बोलिए
bolie
speak

लिखिए
likhie
write

Note that with "*...ie*", the actions "*de*", "*kar*", "*le*", and "*pi*" become "*deej*", "*keej*", "*leej*", and "*peej*" respectively:

दीजिए
deejie
give

कीजिए
keejie
do

लीजिए

leejie

take

पीजिए

peejie

drink

A neutral alternative can be formed by adding the helper "...*na*" to an action; this instruction might appear in recipes or notices etc:

बोलना

bolna

speak

जाना

jaana

go

To tell someone *not* to do something, use the helpers "*na*" or "*mat*"—which one to use depends on the form of the instruction, as shown below (note that "*bolo*" etc can take either):

मत बोल

mat bol

don't speak

न बोलें

na bolen

don't speak

मत बोलो

mat bolo

don't speak

न बोलो

na bolo

don't speak

न बोलिए

na bolie

don't speak

मत बोलना

mat bolna

don't speak

Emphasising words

The helper "*hi*" has no equivalent translation in English; essentially, it emphasises the object it follows:

आदमी ही देखता है
aadmi hi dekhta hei
the MAN sees ~nobody else sees

This helper also combines with some of the troublemakers we looked at in Chapter Three. For example, with "*hi*", the special forms "*is*" and "*in*" combine into "*isi*" and "*inheen*" respectively, while "*us*" and "*un*" become "*usi*" and "*unheen*". This sounds complicated, but imagine that you are still simply saying "*is hi*" or "*un hi*" etc. You will automatically roll the two words together in normal speech anyway, so it is easier to consider this a specific feature of *written* Hindi only:

इसी पर
isi par
on IT ~ "*is hi*"

उसी पर
usi par
on IT ~ "*us hi*"

इन्हीं पर
inheen par
on THEM ~ "*in hi*"

उन्हीं पर
unheen par
on THEM ~ "*un hi*"

Note that the latter two special forms end in nasal *N*s.

Dropping words

Words are often omitted when the meaning of a phrase is obvious; for example, the helper *"ko"* is often dropped when denoting a location:

वह भारत जाता है

vo Bhaarat ~~ko~~ jaata hei
he goes to India

मैं घर जाता हूं

mein ghar ~~ko~~ jaata hoon
I go to the house

The helper *"hei"* is often dropped when *"naheen"* appears:

औरत नहीं जाती

aurat naheen jaati ~~hei~~
the woman does not go

वह नहीं बोलता

vo naheen bolta ~~hei~~
he does not speak

Note that this is the one instance in which the helper *"...ta"* can add *N* when more than one woman is denoted—just as *"tha"* and *"...a"* are able to do:

वे नहीं बोलती हैं

vo naheen bolti hein
they do not speak

वे नहीं बोलतीं

vo naheen bolteen
they do not speak

Phrases with "*ne*"

If an action appears with the helper "*...a*", you must add "*ne*" after the performer of the action:

आदमी ने एक औरत देखी

*aadmi **ne** ek aurat dekhi*
the man saw a woman

You may have noticed that although we are saying "the man", the action is acting as though it was a *woman* who saw something, not "the man". Think of it as if the helpers that come after objects "block" those objects from being the performer of an action; since "*aadmi*" is appearing with the helper "*ne*", it cannot act as the performer of the action. Therefore, the only remaining object available to act as the performer of the action is "*aurat*":

आदमी ने एक औरत देखी

aadmi ne ek aurat dekhi
the man saw a woman

Take a look at these other examples of objects being forced to act as though they were the performer of an action; in each, the object that is affected by the action is acting as if it were performing the action:

औरत ने एक आदमी देखा

aurat ne ek aadmi dekha
the woman saw a man

हम ने घर देखा

ham ne ghar dekha
we saw the house

उस ने घर देखे

us ne ghar dekhe

he saw the houses

आदमी ने एक लड़की देखी

aadmi ne ek larki dekhi

the man saw a girl

If an action cannot affect an object, as with actions such as "go", "jump", "run", "swim" (there is no object that "is gone", "is jumped", "is run", or "is swam" etc), *ne* is not used:

आदमी गया

aadmi gaya

the man went

यह उछली

ye uchali

she jumped

Previously, I described how "*ko*" is often used to denote objects that are affected by actions:

वह औरत को देखता है

*vo aurat **ko** dekhta hei*

he sees the woman

आदमी मुझे देखता है

*aadmi **mujhe** dekhta hei*

the man sees me

Given that helpers block objects from acting as the performer of an action, when "*ko*" appears, there is no available object to act as the performer. In this instance, the action appears in its default form:

उस ने एक औरत देखी

us ne ek aurat dekhi

he saw a woman

उस ने औरत को देखा

*us ne aurat ko dekh**a***

he saw the woman

उस ने घर देखे

us ne ghar dekhe

he saw the houses

उस ने उन घरों को देखा

us ne un gharon ko dekha

he saw those houses

Note that the helper *"ne"* is one of those helpers that make an object act as though it denoted more than one thing:

लड़के ने इसे देखा

larke ne ise dekha

the boy saw him

लड़कों ने इसे देखा

larkon ne ise dekha

the boys saw him

There is just one more set of rules to learn about *"ne"*. Before the helper *"ne"*, the special forms of some of the troublemakers from Chapter Three undergo further changes; for example, the special form *"in"* changes to *"inhon"*, and a similar change occurs with *"un"*, *"kin"*, and *"jin"* (all these special forms end in nasal *N*s):

इन्हों ने एक औरत देखी

inhon *ne ek aurat dekhi*

they saw a woman

उन्हों ने एक औरत देखी

unhon *ne ek aurat dekhi*

they saw a woman

किन्हों ने औरत को देखा?

Kinhon *ne aurat ko dekha?*

Who saw the woman? ~which people?

वे आदमी **जिन्हों** ने औरत को देखी
*vo aadmi **jinhon** ne aurat ko dekha*
the men who saw the woman

In contrast, the special forms *"mujh"* and *"tujh"* actually revert back to their original forms:

मैं ने आदमी को देखा   तू ने आदमी को देखा
***mein** ne aadmi ko dekha*   ***tu** ne aadmi ko dekha*
I saw the man   you saw the man

Actions denoted by phrases

In Hindi, as in English, most actual actions are indicated by one word: "do", "give", "eat", "run", "speak", etc:

कर   दे
kar   *de*
do   give

However, a large number of actions in Hindi are actually denoted by a whole phrase:

वह काम करता है   मैं मदद देता हूं
vo kaam karta hei   *mein madad deta hoon*
he works   I help

In phrases like these, an action appears with an additional word. Do not worry about the meaning of this additional word; you just need to learn the elevated meaning of the phrase:

he works

vo kaam karta hei > he does "*kaam*"

he helps

vo madad deta hei > he gives "*madad*"

Some more Hindi phrases that can be translated by a single action in English are listed below:

वह शुरू करता है
vo shuru karta hei
he begins

वह मदद देता है
vo madad deta hei
he helps

वह साफ़ करता है
vo saaf karta hei
he cleans

वह इकट्ठा करता है
vo ikaṭṭha karta hei
he collects

वह शिकायत करता है
vo shikaayat karta hei
he complains

वह जारी रहिता है
vo jaari rahta hei
it continues

वह ख़तम होता है
vo khatam hota hei
it finishes

वह माफ़ करता है
vo maaf karta hei
he forgives

वह इस से शादी करता है
vo is se shaadi karta hei
he marries her

वह तैयार करता है
vo teiyaar karta hei
he prepares

वह वादा करता है
vo vaada karta hei
he promises

मैं उसकी मरम्मत करता हूं
mein us ki maramat karta hoon
I repair it

वह आराम करता है
vo aaraam karta hei
he rests

वह काम करता है
vo kaam karta hei
he works

Always remember that you are saying a phrase—not an action. Grammar books sometimes present phrases like this as a special type of action: "*kaam karna*" – "to work", "*madad dena*" – "to help", "*shuru karna*" – "to begin", but in my view, these are just phrases that consist of an object (or another type of word) followed by an action; you should always remember the literal translation: "do '*kaam*'", "give '*madad*'", and "do '*shuru*'". (The reason why I am saying this is important is extremely technical, but if you are interested, look at the following example:

औरत काम करती है
aurat kaam karti hei
the woman works

Here, we are essentially saying "the woman *'kaam'* does". If we wanted to say "the woman *worked*", we would say:

औरत ने काम किया
aurat ne kaam kiya
the woman worked

If we considered *"kaam karna"* a syntactic whole—i.e. that *"kaam"* was somehow a part of the "verb"—it would not be immediately obvious either that *"kaam"* could function as the performer of the action or that *"ne"* was even necessary; in linguistic terms, it would not be clear that *"kaam"* could be the "object" in the Hindi "ergative" system.)

Adding detail to actions

More detail about how an action happened can be denoted by using one action after another; for example, using the action *"ja"* after another action denotes a change of state:

वह सोया
vo soya
he slept

वह सो गया
*vo so **gaya***
he fell asleep

The same actual action is denoted—"sleep", "read", "see", "eat", etc—but by adding *"ja"*, you can emphasise the change of state from one situation (being awake) to another (being asleep). Note that in the this example, we do have a convenient English translation—"he *fell asleep*"—but this is not always the case. Phrases like this are used all the time by Hindi speakers—and not just with "*ja*". For example, the action "*parr*" is used when the action was unexpected, sudden, and unpreventable:

वह हंसा
vo hansa
he laughed

वह हंस पड़ा
*vo hans **paṛa***
he burst out laughing

The action "*nikal*" is also used when the action was unexpected and sudden, but also when the action involved movement out or away from a location:

वह उछला
vo uchala
he jumped

वह उछल निकला
*vo uchal **nikala***
he jumped away

The action "*de*" is used when an action was done for someone else, while "*le*" is used when an action was done for oneself:

मैं ने इस किताब को पढ़ा
mein ne is kitaab ko paṛha
I read this book

मैं ने इस किताब को पढ़ दिया
*mein ne is kitaab ko paṛh **diya***
I read this book ~read aloud

मैं ने इस किताब को पढ़ **लिया**
*mein ne is kitaab ko paṛh **liya***
I read this book ~for myself

You may have noticed that all these elevations denote variations of "he slept", "he laughed", "he ran", etc. Elevations like these are mostly used when talking about the past like this—or when giving instructions. They are not used in negative phrases:

वह सो गया
vo so gaya
he fell asleep

वह नहीं सोया
vo naheen soya
he did not sleep

As with the phrases with "*ne*" that were described in the previous section, always remember that you are saying a phrase—not an action. The phrase "*vo so gaya*" is essentially "he sleep went"; likewise, "*vo seb kha gaya*" is essentially "he the apple eat went". If you bear this in mind, you should not have a problem deciding whether to use the helper "*ne*":

उस ने सेब खा लिया
us ne seb kha liya
he ate the apple

वह सेब खा गया
***vo** seb kha gaya*
he ate the apple

More special forms

In Chapter Three, I described the special forms of the actions "*de*", "*kar*", "*le*", and "*pi*":

आदमी ने दिया
aadmi ne diya
the man gave

आदमी ने किया
aadmi ne kiya
the man did

आदमी ने लिया
aadmi ne liya
the man took

आदमी ने पिया
aadmi ne piya
the man drank

As these forms all contain the letters *IY*; when talking about women, you would end up with *IYEe*. As this is difficult to pronounce, this sequence of sounds has been condensed into *Ee*. Again, think of this more as a change in written Hindi only, since in normal speech, you would pronounce *IYEe* as something like a simple *Ee* anyway:

औरत ने पानी पिया
aurat ne paani piya
the woman drank water

आदमी ने चाय पी
aadmi ne caay pi
the man drank tea

मैं ने किताब पढ़ दी
mein ne kitaab paṛh di
I read the book ~read aloud

मैं ने किताब पढ़ ली

*mein ne kitaab paṛh **li***
I read the book ~for myself

मैं ने किताबें पढ़ दीं

*mein ne kitaaben paṛh **deen***
I read the books ~read aloud

मैं ने किताबें पढ़ लीं

*mein ne kitaaben paṛh **leen***
I read the books ~for myself

आदमी औरत से शादी करता है

aadmi aurat se shaadi karta hei
the man marries the woman

आदमी ने औरत से शादी की

*aadmi ne aurat se **shaadi** ki*
the man married the woman

(The reason why I have not discussed this change till now is that as you can see from the examples, these changes—by default—only occur in phrases with "*ne*", since with "*de*", "*kar*", "*le*" and "*pi*", there is always going to be something that is "given", "done", "taken", or "drunk"; therefore, they occur only when the second object in a phrase can act like the performer of an action, as in the second example above. Likewise, as they often occur in the types of phrases detailed in the previous two sections in this chapter, any illustrative examples would have been confusing.)

"and"

The helper "*aur*" – "and" is used just as it is in English:

आदमी और औरतें
aadmi aur auraten
men and women

वह लाल और नीला है
vo laal aur neela hei
it is red and blue

वह वहां जाता है और बोलता है
vo vahaan jaata hei aur bolta hei
he goes there and speaks

In the last example, "*aur*" appears between two phrases; in this instance, an alternative way of saying "and" is to use instead the helper "*...kar*", as follows:

वह वहां जाकर बोलता है
vo vahaan jaakar bolta hei
he goes there and speaks

Remember that there is also an action "*kar*"; in order to avoid two words that sound the same appearing next to each other, the helper "*...kar*" becomes "*...ke*" with this action:

वह इसे करके जाता है
vo ise karke jaata hei
he does it and goes

Finally, note that in phrases with *"ne"*, it is always the second action that determines whether *"ne"* is used:

उस ने वहां जाकर किताब पढ़ी

*us **ne** vahaan jaakar kitaab **pa**r**hi***

he went there and read a book

वह औरत को देखकर वहां गया

*vo aurat ko dekhkar vahaan **gaya***

he saw the woman and went there

Different doers

The following elevations are like the example discussed at the beginning of the chapter (*"mujhe kitaab pasand hei"* – "to me the book *'pasand'* is"); essentially, in phrases like these, the person who is performing the action in English is not the same as the person who is performing the action in Hindi. Hindi has a lot of phrases like this; there are several below:

मुझे किताब चाहिए

mujhe kitaab caahie

I need the book

मुझे किताब पसंद है

mujhe kitaab pasand hei

I like the book

मुझे पता नहीं है

mujhe pata naheen hei

I do not know

इसे भूक लगती है

ise bhook lagti hei

he feels hungry

मुझे याद नहीं
mujhe yaad naheen
I don't remember

वहां जाने में दो दिन लगते हैं
vahaan jaane men do din lagte hein
it takes two days to get there

Other elevations

The following are some other elevations that you may find useful:

कितने बजे हैं?
Kitne baje hein?
What time is it?

पांच बजे हैं
paanc baje hein
it's five o'clock

किसका क़लम?
kis ka kalam?
whose pen? ~one owner

किनका क़लम?
kin ka kalam?
whose pen? ~multiple owners

कौन सी औरत?
kaun si aurat?
which woman?

कितने आदमी?
kitne aadmi?
how many men?

आपकी बहिन, पिता, और भाई
*aap ki bahin, **pita**, aur **bhai***
your sister, father, and brother

वह यहां बैठा है
vo yahaan beiṭha hei
he **is sitting** here ~when describing positions

Of course, there are many more elevations you will need to learn. As you may have guessed from the examples in this section, it is often the case that some of the most frequently used phrases in a language can be quite complex elevations. If you only ever learn lots of abstract rules and memorise lots of words, you will be able to say a huge number of phrases; however, when you start to learn elevations and subsequently use them, you really begin to "use" the language in the proper sense—because you will be manipulating both words and abstract rules at the same time. For the technically minded, imagine that your mouth and ears are the basic "hardware" you use to produce and understand a language, the rules you have been learning are the "operating system" of that language, and the words of the language are your "files". In this analogy, elevations would be the "software" you use to actually do anything but the most basic tasks. Elevations are fundamental when producing and understanding a language.

Chapter Six: Hindi Script

Now that we have discussed the basic, elementary, and intermediate rules of Hindi, including "grammatical" rules in the traditional sense and rules about pronunciation, and the words and elevations in the previous two chapters, we are ready to look at the rules that govern how to read and write Hindi script.

The challenges of Hindi script

The script used to write Hindi is often praised as one that is scientific, efficient, and simple to learn. I believe this is because it is *phonetic*, in that there is more or less a one-to-one correspondence between the sounds of the language and the letters used to represent them. In contrast, when encountering a new word in Urdu, which uses a modified version of Arabic script, you can never be completely sure how that word is pronounced, in a way that you can be with scripts that do represent more of the sounds of a given word, such as languages like English and French (albeit inconsistently), Spanish and Russian (fairly regularly)—and Hindi. This does not mean to say that these scripts are any "better" than Arabic script—it just means that in terms of working out how to pronounce new words, these scripts would probably be easier for a learner.

Nevertheless, in my opinion, there are two reasons why Hindi script is just as challenging (in its own way) as the script used for Urdu (and Arabic and Persian etc). First, in my view, Hindi script is a little *too* scientific—at least for the learner. What I mean by this is the way the script is traditionally described reads like a linguistics textbook description of phonetic symbols; for example, "aspirated" consonants in Hindi script (which in this book, are simply consonants that are described as appearing directly before the letter *H*) are always presented as separate letters in their own right—as are the "retroflex" consonants (*D*, *R*, and *T*, pronounced with the tongue touching the roof of the mouth). This is phonetically accurate, but in my view, it simply multiplies the number of unfamiliar symbols the learner must memorise. Considering "aspirated" consonants as simply instances of a letter followed by *H* (as in fact Urdu script presents them) is in my view more learner friendly.

The second reason is that for such a scientific and logical system, Hindi script is also extremely quirky! You only have to look at the scores of different "conjunct" forms (along with their exceptions in individual words) to see that the system is actually fundamentally complex in a way that Urdu script, with its essential "core" of letter shapes, is not. It is precisely these complexities and inconsistencies that have made an elegant transliteration system impossible; the English letters used in this book to represent Hindi script unavoidably contain differentiating marks such as dots below consonants, hyphens, and underlined letters for "conjunct" forms. And of course, the positive reputation Hindi script enjoys implies that other scripts are somehow "lesser" because of their redundant letters and lack of a one-to-one correspondence between sounds and letters. Nevertheless, if you approach Hindi with a background in Urdu (as I did), it is tempting to view Hindi script as somewhat overly methodical—yet inexplicably complex at the same time!

In any event, you could argue that Hindi script is certainly far less efficient than Urdu script, because you have to use more symbols to represent individual sounds and decode more of those symbols when reading; after Urdu, you may consider writing *all* the letters of a given word a bit of a chore! Of course, this is an exaggeration; but I would like to counter the claims that are implied in some resources (and defend Urdu script from an implied inferiority). Just be aware when you buy a book on Hindi script, and the first chapter is all about how amazingly scientific and easy it is, skip ahead to the many pages describing the various "conjuncts", and you will gain a more realistic view.

Leaving Hindi script till last

Many books and classes on Hindi begin with a discussion of the script; in my view, this is a more difficult way of progressing than approaching the script after you have learned both lots of words and how the language is actually structured. The simple reason for this is that you now know lots of words and rules in Hindi (just as a native-speaking child does when he or she first begins to learn how to read and write); therefore, when you do encounter written words, you will be less intimidated by the unfamiliar script, and you will not have to try to decode the language itself while also decoding an unfamiliar script. The rules you have learned have already been "mapped" in your brain using the letters of the English alphabet. Nobody would expect children to learn how to read words in their first language before they can actually speak that language to the level they are able to speak it when they first start school and begin to learn to read and write; therefore, why expect adults to do this? Therefore, with this in mind, let's look at how Hindi script works.

Letters

The following letters of Hindi script correspond to the following letters used in this book:

ब	च	द	फ़	ग	ह
B	*C*	*D*	*F*	*G*	*H*

ज	क	ल	म	न	प
J	*K*	*L*	*M*	*N*	*P*

र	स	त	व	य	ज़
R	*S*	*T*	*V*	*Y*	*Z*

The following letters of the Hindi script correspond to the versions of *D*, *R*, and *T* in which the tongue touches the roof of the mouth:

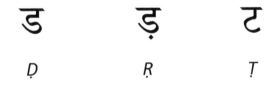

ड	ड़	ट
Ḍ	*Ṛ*	*Ṭ*

Vowels are written as additional marks that are added to the previous consonant, as follows—note that *A* is not written in this instance (as in the first example below):

ब	बा	बि	बी	बु
BA	BAa	BI	BEe	BU

बू	बे	बै	बो	बौ
BOo	BE	BEi	BO	BAu

When there is no previous consonant (such as after another vowel or at the beginning of a word), vowels appear as follows:

अ	आ	इ	ई	उ
A	Aa	I	Ee	U

ऊ	ए	ऐ	ओ	औ
Oo	E	Ei	O	Au

This is the basic system for writing in Hindi script. There are of course some additional rules that apply, and these are discussed in the sections below. Note that the examples used will manifest features of the script you have not yet learned; as you work through, simply focus on the relevant part of the example only.

Combinations

Most of the time, when two letters come together, the two letters combine into one new form. We have already encountered this; as you learned in the previous section, when a vowel appears after a consonant, both "combine" into a new form (I said that the vowel appears as "additional marks"—this is simply an alternative way of describing the same process):

किसान
kisaan
farmer

सेब
seb
apple

However, the same process can also occur with consonants. Of particular note are combinations in which the second letter is *H*; these appear as follows:

BH   भ

CH   छ

DH   ध

GH	घ
JH	झ
KH	ख
PH	फ
SH	श
TH	थ
ḌH	ढ
ṚH	ढ़
ṬH	ठ

भालू
bhaalu
bear

छत
chat
roof

दूध
doodh
milk

घर
ghar
home

झील
jheel
lake

मुख
mukh
face

फूल
phool
flower

हाथ
haath
hand

भालू
ḍhang
bear

वह पढ़े गा
vo paṛhe ga
he will read

पीठ
peeṭh
back

Note that as you might expect, the combination *SH* is pronounced as in English—like the SH of "ship":

शेर
sher
lion

देश
desh
country

The letter *N* also combines with other consonants. Whenever a letter *N* appears directly before another consonant, it "combines" into a dot above the previous letter, as follows:

कंबल
kanbal
blanket

रंग
rang
colour

You may also see a "moon" shape below the dot that denotes *N*; you do not need to write this yourself, and it can be ignored. This shape is used to distinguish the dot that denotes a letter *N* and another type of dot that denotes a nasal vowel. The latter takes a "moon" shape where possible, while the former does not. In this book, I have not attempted to distinguish these two symbols, as in practice, you do not have to write it, and it does not realistically affect everyday pronunciation:

कंबल

kanbal
blanket ~the letter *N*

वहाँ

vahaan
there ~nasal vowel

In some words, you may also encounter the letter *N* in an alternative combination, as follows:

हिंदी

Hindi
Hindi

हिन्दी

Hindi
Hindi

This is also how words like *"inhen"*, *"unhen"*, *"kinhen"*, etc are always written:

आप उन्हें किताब देते हैं

aap unhen kitaab dete hein
you give the book to them

वे आदमी जिन्हें आप किताब देते हैं

vo aadmi jinhen aap kitaab dete hein
the men to whom you give the book

आप किताब किन्हें देते हैं

Aap kitaab kinhen dete hein?
To whom do you give the book?

Like *N* and *H*, the letter *R* also combines with other consonants in an important way. When it is the first consonant in a combination, *R* appears as an additional mark above the following consonant, as follows:

दर्द	धर्म
dard	*dharm*
pain	religion

When *R* is the second consonant in a combination, it appears as an additional mark below the following consonant, as follows:

उम्र	अंग्रेज़ी
umr	*Angrezi*
age	English

In addition to *H*, *N*, and *R*, other consonants may also combine in different ways. One major type of combination occurs when two consonants come together that are represented in Hindi script by letters that include vertical lines. In this instance, simply remove the vertical line of the first consonant and add whatever remains of the letter to the following consonant. This sounds complicated, but is actually very straightforward—take a look at the following examples:

प्यार	सस्ता
pyaar	*sasta*
love	cheap

डिब्बा	बच्चा
ḍibba	*bacca*
box	child

Note that when the first consonant of such a combination is *K* or *F*, these letters keep their vertical line (since their core shape extends across that line):

क्यों	दफ़्तर
kyon	*daftar*
why	office

However, there are combinations of letters that do not follow the previous rule. This book does not attempt to represent them all, but some others you will encounter in this book include:

DY	द्य
TR	त्र

_TT_   द्द

_TT_   त्त

TTH   ड्ढ

विद्यार्थी   सत्रह
vidyaarthi   _satrah_
student   seventeen

छुट्टी   कुत्ता
chuṭṭi   _kutta_
holiday   dog

अट्ठाईस
aṭṭhaees
28

When combinations are simply too complex to write or type easily, the following symbol can be used to denote that there is no vowel after the letter above it:

छुट्टी   छुट्‍टी
chuṭṭi   >   _chuṭṭi_
holiday   holiday

सत्रह		सत्रह
satrah	>	*satrah*
seventeen		seventeen

When you are learning words from the list in Chapter Four, you can presume that all combinations with vowels, all combinations in which the second letter is *H* or *Y*, all instances of *N* before a consonant, all combinations involving *R*, and all doubled letters (*CC, SS, NN*, etc) combine as per the rules described above:

हिसाबि	*hisaab*	account
भालू	*bhaalu*	bear
प्याला	*pyaala*	cup
कंबल	*kanbal*	blanket
मुर्गी	*murgi*	chicken
बच्चा	*bacca*	child

However, any other combination has been indicated by underlining the specific letters that make up that combination—this was necessary because in some instances, these letters combined, and in others, they did not combine. This means it is necessary to learn on a word-by-word basis which sequences of letters combine and which do not. This is one of the major features of Hindi script that make it challenging:

बिस्तर	*bistar*	bed
गोश्त	*gosht*	meat
दफ्तर	*daftar*	office

Indeed, in Chapter Four, I have often had to use hyphens to clarify the Hindi script spelling; in the following examples, a hyphen indicates that an expected combination does not in fact occur—or otherwise clarifies the pronunciation of the word:

जानवार	*jaan-vaar*	animal
परदा	*par-da*	curtain
इकहत्तर	*ik-hattar*	71
तेईस	*te-ees*	23

Other changes

There are some other changes that certain letters undergo, whether in combination with other letters or not. First, the very common words *"ye"* and *"vo"* are written as if they were *"yah"* and *"vah"* when denoting one thing and *"ye"* and *"ve"* when denoting more than one thing (you may also hear these forms in spoken Hindi):

यह	वह
ye / yah	*vo / vah*
this	that

ये	वे
ye	*vo / ve*
these	those

Instances of *"aap ka"*, *"is ka"*, *"us ka"*, *"in ka"*, *"kis ka"*, etc, which I said in Chapter Three are not combined, are actually written as one word in Hindi script:

इसका सेब

is ka seb

his apple ~ *"iska seb"*

आपका सेब

aap ka seb

your apple ~ *"aapka seb"*

As described in Chapter One, the vowels *Aa*, *Ee*, and *Oo* are written *A*, *I*, and *U* respectively—unless followed by a consonant:

प्याला

pyaala

cup ~ *"pyaalaa"*

बिल्ली

billi

cat ~ *"billee"*

आलू

aalu

potato ~ *"aaloo"*

भाई

bhai

brother ~ *"bhaaee"*

However, in a similar fashion to *"ye"* and *"vo"*, what should be *Aa*, *Ee* , or *Oo* in some very common words (as denoted in the system used in this book) is actually *A*, *I*, or *U* respectively. It is simpler just to learn these words as isolated examples:

चेन्नई

Cennai

Chennai

मुम्बई

Mumbai

Mumbai

मई	कई
Mai	*kai*
May	several

क्योंकि	कि
kyonki	*ki*
because	that

न
na
neither

Similarly, note that *I* followed by *E* is written this way:

के लिए	आदमी को बोलना चाहिए
ke lie	*aadmi ko bolna caahie*
for	the man should speak

Note the spelling of two of the special actions mentioned in Chapter Three:

वह गया	वह गई
vo gaya	*vo gayi*
he went	she went

वे गए	वे गईं
vo gaye	*vo gayeen*
they went	they went

वह हुआ

vo hua

he became

वह हुई

vo hui

she became

वे हुए

vo hue

they became

वे हुईं

vo hueen

they became

Many words in Hindi were originally adopted into the language from Persian; in some words of Persian origin, you may see the following letters with a dot below them:

क़ालीन

kaaleen

carpet

ग़लत

galti

mistake

ख़बर

khabar

news

This dot is used to denote letters that originally corresponded to the Persian letters ق, غ, and خ. The first two letters are pronounced like *K* and *G* respectively, but further back in the throat, while the third is pronounced like the CH of Scottish "lo**ch**". However, many Hindi speakers do not distinguish these letters from "normal" *K*, *G*, and *KH*—likewise, in writing, the dots are inconsistently applied.

The same process seems to be taking place for the other sounds borrowed from Persian—*F* and *Z*—which are also often pronounced as the Hindi letters under which the dots appear: *PH* and *J* respectively. In the system used in this book, I have not included the dotted versions of *K*, *G*, and *Kh* letters as independent letters; however, I have maintained the letters *F* and *Z*, if only because these sounds also occur in English. Hindi has also adopted many words from Sanskrit—especially as language planners seek to distance the language from its sister, Urdu (though of course, English is now the main "threat" to any linguistic "purity"). In some words of Sanskrit origin, the letter *N* and the combination *SH* may appear differently. Take a look at the last letter of the following examples:

उदाहरण

udaaharan

example

विशेष

vishesh

special

Likewise, in words of Sanskrit origin, the combination *RI* can appear as a "C"-shape below a previous consonant—or as ऋ in any other positon:

संस्कृत

Sanskrit

Sanskrit

ऋण

rin

debt

Numbers and punctuation

In addition to letters, there are two additional sets of symbols that are used in Hindi script; these are the symbols for numbers and punctuation. The following symbols are used to denote numbers (though they are rapidly being replaced by the ones used in English):

१	२	३	४	५
1	*2*	*3*	*4*	*5*

६	७	८	९	०
6	*7*	*8*	*9*	*0*

१८९०	८५५ सेब
1890	*855 seb*
1890	855 apples

Punctuation symbols are much the same as in English, except that a full stop is often a short vertical line:

क्या आप जाते हैं?	पानी, दूध, शराब।
Kya aap jaate hein?	*Paani, doodh, sharaab.*
Do you go?	Water, milk, wine.

Typing Hindi online

When typing Hindi online, many speakers use the letters of the English alphabet instead of Hindi script because it is still often difficult to write in certain scripts online. If you type Hindi using the system of English letters used in this book, you should be understood well enough. However, it would be advisable to make some the following changes so that Hindi speakers can more easily understand what you are trying to say. For example, the letter *C* should be typed CH:

चाय

chaay

tea

चावल

chaaval

rice

All dots, hyphens, and underlined letters should of course be avoided—though you may see the versions of *D*, *R*, and *T* that are pronounced with the tongue touching the roof of the mouth typed in capitals:

टिकट

TikaT

ticket

लड़का

laRka

boy

Some speakers may not type any nasal *N*:

मैं घर में हूं

mei ghar me hu

I am in the house

वे यहां हों गे

vo yaha ho ge

they will be here

The letter *V* is often typed W:

वह जवान है

wo jawaan hei

he is young

वह वहां है

wo waha hei

he is there

At the end of a word, *Aa*, *Ee*, and *Oo* may be typed in full:

अच्छा लड़का

achchhaa laRkaa

the good boy

आदमी आलू खाता है

aadmee aaloo khaataa hei

the man eats the potato

Similarly, *E* often becomes AY, *Ei* often becomes AI, and *A* can appear as U or even E:

लड़के वहां हैं

leRkay wuhaa hai

the boys are there

हम घर में हैं

hum ghar may hai

we are in the house

Conclusion

Congratulations on completing this book on Hindi grammar. The question you might be asking yourself now is: "Where do I go from here?" There are many different theories about how best to study a language. In my view, they all involve at some point learning words, rules, and elevations and improving your speaking, listening, writing, and reading skills until you can understand and produce the language with your desired degree of fluency and/or accuracy. Hopefully, this section will give you some pointers about how to do that.

Where are the "advanced" rules?

The aim of this book was to develop your knowledge of Hindi to the extent that you might never need to consult another grammar book again or even attend another formal Hindi class. This is because you can classify anything you encounter in Hindi from now on in terms of the rules you have learned; if you encounter a new word, you will be able to classify it as an object, helper, descriptor, or action, and you will know how to use it accordingly. Similarly, if you encounter a phrase that does not seem to make sense when you translate it literally, you will know that you have encountered an elevation and that you need to learn a single example of it.

Just as you will encounter additional words and elevations, you will of course still encounter additional rules; this book has not covered everything, and there are some very specific rules about pronunciation (for example, different Indian accents). Equally, there are more rules about Hindi script (for example, the features of handwritten Hindi). There are even more "grammatical" rules in the traditional sense of the word, though you will be able to classify most of these as elevations. I've called all these rules "advanced", and have not attempted to include them in this book.

Partly, this is because this book was written for beginners and is not designed to be an encyclopedia of every single rule in the language; mostly though, I have not tried to include every single rule in Hindi because the most important thing to remember about advanced rules is that you do not need to worry so much about them! The point at which you might want to take more notice of advanced rules that cover very specific details of technical points about grammar or pronunciation etc is the point at which you can deal with them perfectly well without either this book or any other grammar book! You now have a mental structure that you can use to organise any new information you encounter; however, if you subsequently hear or read something that sounds incredibly complex, just ignore it and don't come back to it until your Hindi is at the level that someone would be able to explain it to you in Hindi—in other words, so long as you understand the gist of the conversations you have or the movies you watch, everything is fine! Don't let a very specific little rule interrupt the conversation you are having at your family dinner or the plot of your favourite Indian soap opera.

Finally, remember that all the labels used in this book ("words"— "objects", "helpers", "actions", "descriptors"—"phrases", "rules", and "elevations") are merely mental tools to organise a language. They are very much arbitrary, and you should use them in a way that you think is the most appropriate—and not necessarily in the way that I suggest. Likewise, labels such as "noun", "pronoun" "verb", etc that you will encounter in language resources generally are just as arbitrary, and you should not feel you have to use them in the way the author suggests (or even insists, in some cases). For example, you might prefer to consider phrases such as "*ghar ki taraf*" – "toward the house" as an object ("*ghar*" – "house") with a helper ("*ki taraf*" – "toward"), as I have done:

ghar [ki taraf] > [toward] the house

However, you could equally consider phrases such as this as two objects ("*ghar*" – "house" and "*taraf*" – "direction") joined by a helper ("*ka*") to produce an elevation ("*ghar ki taraf*" – "the direction of the house", elevated to "toward the house"):

toward
ghar ki taraf > ~~the direction of~~ the house

Either way is absolutely acceptable and fundamentally "correct". Despite what you might infer from other grammar books, there is no definitive analysis in grammar; simply use the "tools" that both best describe the phrase and best fit the language as a whole. If an analysis allows you to understand and produce correct phrases in any given language, then that analysis is itself just as correct as any found in a peer-reviewed journal.

What do I need to do now?

As I mentioned, you probably won't need to attend any more formal classes or read any more grammar books. What you definitely do need to do is learn more words and elevations, practise recognising and using the rules in this book, and practise your speaking, listening, writing, and reading skills. Fortunately, there is a very easy way to do all these things at the same time: simply do things in Hindi! This may sound like a very obvious point, but I am often surprised at how even people who have learned languages before come to a weekly class and expect to improve when they neither attempt to speak the target language in that class nor do anything in that language between classes. Of course, time is an issue for everyone, and it is much easier actually doing things in Hindi if you have Indian friends or family, have hours free to spend practising, or live in one of the many areas in which South Asian people have settled in substantial numbers. Whatever your situation, if you do want to learn a language, at some point you need to actually do things in that language.

So what do I mean by "doing things" in Hindi? (I am presuming that you do not live in India or a Hindi-speaking environment; if you do, the answer to this question should be obvious: go outside, have conversations, and read and write stuff!) Despite what I said before, don't quit your weekly Hindi class or give away your grammar books. Use the time in class to actually have conversations in Hindi—at least, as much as the teacher will allow. Remember that your teacher will probably still think it is his or her job to teach you grammar. If you are able to use your class time to actually speak Hindi, don't worry if you are only ever able to speak with other learners. Speaking with your fellow learners is a great way of improving your fluency because other learners will usually use words and elevations you understand;

they will also speak quite slowly and carefully—unlike most native speakers! Also, use your grammar books to practise reading—so long as you remember not to get distracted by the complex descriptions of rules. Remember, it is not the rules that are necessarily complicated, it's how they are described that is complicated. In particular, don't be distracted by the grammatical labels used; the tendency to resort to arcane terminology is particularly common in grammar books of lesser-taught languages like Hindi, which is ironic really because the need for simpler labels is all the more important! Just use your grammar books to practise your reading and to pick up new words and elevations.

However, neither speaking Hindi in class nor using your grammar books to practise your reading is what I mean by "doing things" in Hindi. What I mean is that you should try as much as possible to do all the other things you do on a regular basis—work, watch TV, write emails, browse the internet, play computer games, talk to your children, etc—in Hindi. Admittedly, doing all your everyday activities in Hindi is easier if you live in a Hindi-speaking environment, but there is absolutely no obstacle to doing so if you have access to modern technology. Go on the internet and watch free Hindi-language movies or TV programmes. Read websites in Hindi. Join online Hindi chatrooms. Go on social networking sites to find a local South Asian society or club and attend their regular events. Participate in a language exchange with Hindi-speaking students at your local university (have an hour of conversation in English, followed by an hour in Hindi, or otherwise help them with their English by proofreading their work). Make a prank phonecall to a swimming pool in Delhi, asking about opening times! Switch the language of your web browser, phone, and favourite computer game to Hindi (if possible). Order Hindi books online (especially ones with translations in English) and cheap Indian magazines and newspapers. For extra pronunciation practice, download a Hindi song you like, learn it by heart, and sing it back to yourself as you play it in your car. If you want to know the meaning of a word but don't have a dictionary, type that word into a popular search engine but click on an image search instead of the usual text search; if lots of images of the same thing come back, chances are good that you've discovered the meaning of this word. If you don't know how to pronounce a word you encounter in Hindi script (which will happen a lot), there are websites that list words in different languages, and you can click on these words to hear how they are pronounced. In short, if you have access to the internet, there is no excuse for not "doing things" in Hindi.

Should I record new words, rules, and elevations?

Traditionally, language learners have recorded lists of new words, for example in a notebook or word-processed document (as I have done in Chapter Four). If you do this, I suggest you use a word-processed document because you will then be able to go back and find words more easily, modify the text you have typed, rearrange lists of words to give yourself tests, add colour to divide words into categories or levels of difficulty, and go back and add associated words such as helpers. (Remember that when you encounter a helper, you only need to make a note of what it means and where it goes; is the helper appearing before a descriptor for example, or is the helper being used after and to give meaning to an entire phrase? Ask yourself these questions before making a note of any helper.) Colour is particularly useful for those languages—like Hindi, arguably—that have different types (or "genders") of object and different ways of talking about more than one object for example. For example, typing all "feminine" objects in a red font, all "masculine" objects in blue, and all "neuter" objects in yellow is an obvious advantage, particularly for the visually minded. However, if you do keep lists of new words (or elevations or rules for that matter), there comes a point at which your lists become so huge that they are unmanageable. Languages are "information heavy"; essentially, knowledge of a language is a huge mass of information in your brain, and it soon becomes very inconvenient to externally record this information on paper or screen. For this reason, I suggest that you still use the words, rules, and elevations in this book as a starting point but after that, just record new information directly to the "notebook" of your own brain. If you think about it, unless you plan on writing the most comprehensive and definitive Hindi dictionary or grammar book ever produced, you will have to do this at some point—you will never be able to write down absolutely every new word, rule, or elevation you ever encounter in Hindi, so you might as well start relying solely on your brain sooner rather than later!

Although it might sound counterintuitive, whether you adopt this approach or not, don't worry about forgetting information you have not written down. Being exposed to actual Hindi is like doing a revision test on any artificial list of words, rules, or elevations you might otherwise produce—only better, because you'll be having an authentic conversation while you do so or otherwise practising your language skills in a more natural context. You will automatically be "revising" the language you actually need precisely because you're *actually* having these conversations, watching these movies, or reading the texts you mostly read etc. That annoying little word you haven't noted down is still part of the language, and it isn't going anywhere; you will encounter it again at some point. Of course, relying on your brain like this does lack the certainty of a written note, but your brain more than makes up for this by the sheer volume of information it can hold (and unlike your notebook or laptop, you can't accidentally leave it behind on the train).

Isn't it wrong to translate new words into English?

In this book, English is used throughout as the "default" basis of comparison; features of Hindi are described only in relation to English and not in relation to abstract grammatical concepts. Equally, the rules of Hindi have been described only to the extent that they differ from English; for example, if the order of certain words in specific phrases is the same as in English, this rule has not usually been explicitly stated. (Similarly, as English speakers, we also have the distinct advantage that if we do not know the word for something, we can usually use the English word and often be understood no matter where we are in the world or what language we are trying to speak—because English is the current global language. This is particularly so with Hindi, given the proliferation of English throughout South Asia.) Presuming that unless you learn otherwise, rules are the same in Hindi as in English reduces the actual amount of rules you have to consciously learn. Similarly, Hindi words have also been given a direct English translation; indeed, the whole notion of "elevations" is based on the existence of a literal translation (however strange) of any Hindi phrase you encounter.

Depending on your experience of language learning, this may be a new approach to you. Modern methods of language teaching tend not to rely so much on the learner's first language. For example, some language theorists believe that you should approach learning new words just as a child who is learning his or her first language does; the word "cat" for example, which is *"billi"* in Hindi, should be approached not with the reasoning that "the word 'cat' is *'billi'* in Hindi" but that "the small furry animal that chases mice is a *'billi'* when we're speaking Hindi". In my opinion, this is a very effective method that may allow you to actually "think" in the language from the start—but only if you have the time (as children do) to wait for a cat to walk by or come up in conversation while your native-speaking friends are around, who comment on the *"billi"* and point to it, before you figure out the spelling of the word when you encounter it two years later in your schoolbook. If you spend 15 years in a Indian school having lessons and playing games with your Hindi-speaking friends, who can't or won't speak English, then this is a viable method.

However, if you have a busy job and little time (like most adults) and are too old to go back to school, then there is a very simple, effective, and alternative way of learning what the word *"billi"* means: just learn *"billi – cat"*. If you do this, you know what the word *"billi"* means, how to pronounce it, how to spell it in Hindi script (if you use the spelling system in this book), how to use it grammatically, and you can guess that it appears in much the same types of phrases as it does in English. Instead of avoiding English, I believe that you already have an amazing resource to help you learn any new language: your first language! This is a resource that will allow you to learn a lot of words, rules, and elevations much more easily and quickly than you would if you relied on abstract grammatical concepts such as "tense" or "person" etc. Of course, when you become more advanced in Hindi and encounter the word *"billi"*, you will automatically think of that small furry animal that chases mice—but don't feel you need to do this when you first begin to learn the language.

I hope you have enjoyed learning Hindi using this book,
and I hope you have found at least some of it useful.
Good luck in your language learning!

Index

Categories

Elevations

Hindi script

Language learning

Traditional grammatical terms